80 recipes

for your...

Pressure Cooker

80 recipes
for your...
Pressure
Cooker

Richard Ehrlich

Photography by Will Heap

Kyle Cathie Ltd

For Emma

First published in Great Britain in 2011 by
Kyle Cathie Limited
23 Howland Street, London W1T 4AY
general.enquiries@kyle-cathie.com
www.kylecathie.com

ISBN 978-1-85626-944-5

10 9 8 7 6 5 4 3 2 1

Text © 2011 Richard Ehrlich
Photography © 2011 Will Heap
Design © 2011 Kyle Cathie Limited

Project editor: Catharine Robertson
Photographer: Will Heap (see page 143 for additional credits)
Designer: Mark Latter/www.bluedragonfly-uk.com
Food stylist: Jane Lawrie
Props stylist: Sue Rowlands
Copy editor: Jan Cutler
Indexer: Alex Corrin
Production: Gemma John

Richard Ehrlich is hereby identified as the author of this
work in accordance with Section 77 of the Copyright,
Designs and Patents Act 1988.

A Cataloguing in Publication record for this title is available
from the British Library.

Printed and bound by Toppan Leefung Printing Ltd in China

contents

introduction

I hate recommending that people buy a new item of cooking equipment. For the pressure cooker, however, I make an exception. This is the most useful thing you can get for your kitchen, no matter how well equipped it may already be.

Pressure cookers have been around for many decades, and maybe that's part of their image problem: they seem to some home cooks like an old-fashioned piece of hardware that your mother or grandmother used. Even if that's true, you shouldn't let that image keep you from embracing these truly remarkable pans. They speed up cooking by a factor of two, three or even four. You can make dishes for midweek dinners that would ordinarily require the leisurely hours of a weekend. And you don't have to compromise at all in quality.

Pressure cookers cook faster than conventional pans because water boils at a higher temperature when it's under pressure. The pressure cooker has a rubber gasket that creates a tight seal around its rim and a clamp that holds the lid tightly in place. Steam can't escape, except through the built-in safety valves, and as the steam builds up inside – typically to a pressure of 15psi (pounds per square inch) – it raises the temperature in the pan to as much as about 125°C (257°F). The pressurised steam cooks much faster than ordinary boiling water.

This speed is a godsend for certain foods. Not for all, of course; things that cook really quickly (especially fish) are not suitable for pressure cooking. But braised meat and poultry, rice, risotto, pulses and some puddings – these were never faster. The reduced cooking times are convenient for you – dinner arrives speedily – and for the environment, because you're using less energy.

If I had my way, every home kitchen would have a pressure cooker. If you don't have one yet, please give it serious thought. And if you do have one, I hope this book will give you some good ideas for putting it to use.

some general points

don't they explode?

I cannot tell a lie: in the old days, when pressure cookers were much more primitive than today's versions, they sometimes sent a geyser of food shooting at (or onto) the ceiling. Never having seen one of these accidents, I don't know why they happened. But I assume it is because the cook removed or loosened the lid when the contents were still under high pressure. Lid goes flying, contents shoot up to the ceiling.

Early pressure cookers did have a safety valve to vent the steam once full pressure was reached, but the valves were fairly primitive and could be tricky to operate. The valves on modern pressure cookers are safer and easier, and multiple safety mechanisms prevent the excessive build-up of steam. They still need occasional attention to make sure the valve isn't blocked – check the manufacturer's instructions – but on safety grounds there is nothing to fear from them.

a question of release

On all the modern pressure cookers that I've seen and used, the lid can be released only when the steam has vented and the pressure has dropped to a safe level. How do you reach that point? There are two ways. One is to let it vent slowly on its own, which takes about ten to fifteen minutes. The other is to open the vent immediately for faster release, producing an amazing whoosh of billowing steam. If you aim the billowing cloud at the splashback on your hob, you can use it to clean off the surface.

That isn't the only reason for deciding whether to vent quickly or slowly. If you leave the vent closed for slow release of steam, the food will continue cooking. In my experience, venting the steam gradually is the equivalent of five minutes of extra cooking time – but without energy use, which is good for the environment and your fuel bills.

But slow release isn't suitable for all dishes. Green vegetables soften with just a few minutes of pressure cooking, and using the slow release would turn them to mush. For braised vegetables (such as the spring greens on page 124), this is no bad thing. For al dente vegetables, fast release is essential. In all the recipes in this book I specify which venting method to use.

There's another reason to use immediate venting of steam, at least for certain dishes. If you are adding other ingredients to a partially cooked dish, immediate release means that you don't lose as much heat from the pan, so the second stage of cooking will be finished sooner. Immediate release also enables you to check whether the dish is finished, and to give it another few minutes without losing too much heat.

Note: you can also speed up the cooling of a pressure cooker by putting it in cold water. I have found no compelling practical use for this method, finding that rapid venting suffices for most purposes.

filling the tank

Whenever you use a pressure cooker, you have to ensure that it isn't filled either too little or too much. Check the instructions that come with your cooker, and *follow them*. This is especially important when it comes to liquid minimums, which are needed to avoid evaporation of the water leading to food catching on the base of the pan. It's also important to avoid overfilling with foods that expand during cooking, such as rice and pulses. As a general rule, you will need to fill the pressure cooker to at least a depth of 5cm. And you shouldn't fill the pan more than halfway with foods that expand greatly. But again, check the manufacturer's instructions.

a word about buying

There are several brands of pressure cooker. I've used lots of them, and I do have a strong preference for those made by Tefal under the name Clipso. I like it for several reasons, especially the use of two twin lugs instead of the single long handle found on many pressure cookers. The lugs minimise storage space and – in my opinion – make lifting easier. The Clipso also has an ingenious detachable timer in the lid which is coupled with a sensor that tells you when the contents of the pot have reached full pressure. When full pressure is reached, the timer starts counting down.

But brand is less important than basic principles. One, do not expect to get your pressure cooker cheap: these are high-quality stainless-steel cooking vessels, and pots of that type always cost money. Two, look at the pressure cooker in a store before you buy it: high-value cookware should always be put through its paces before you shell out your money on it. Three, don't be tempted to buy a smaller pressure cooker even if you don't often cook for a crowd. The minimum size is usually around 4 litres, the maximum around 6.5 litres. Get the bigger one. It gives you far more flexibility, especially when you're having people over to dinner.

steaming

Many pressure cookers are sold with a steamer rack that fits neatly inside the pot. If yours doesn't have one, or if you need more space for either food or a bowl, you can improvise by using something else: one of those folding iris-type steamers, a small roasting rack, or even an all-metal lid from a small saucepan or frying pan.

a note on timing and liquid

Pressure cooking is different from other methods, and it takes a while to get used to. Every pressure cooker comes with instructions on use, and you should read them carefully. This is especially important because no two are exactly alike, and the results that I get in mine may require slightly less or more time to achieve in yours.

If you're in doubt, or while you're in the learning phase, you shouldn't be afraid to vent the steam immediately and check on doneness. If the food needs more cooking time, just clamp the lid back on and bring it up to full pressure again. This doesn't take long, so you're not wasting much time or energy. After a while, your estimates as to timing will become more accurate. And a cardinal rule: if in doubt, use more liquid. The more you use, the more steam pressure there will be and the faster the food will cook. Excess liquid will be full of flavour; what you don't use immediately will form the basis of another good dish.

what can you cook in a pressure cooker?

I am still trying to figure out the answer to that question, but at the moment the more pertinent question seems to be: what can't you cook? The more I use my pressure cooker, the more I discover its possibilities. Of course, there is one thing the pressure cooker won't do – keep a crisp, browned crust on a piece of meat. But that can't be done in any predominantly moist cooking environment. Excluding that limitation, the list of candidates for pressure is almost endless: meats that you would ordinarily braise; pulses and selected grains; most types of vegetable; complicated dishes and ultra-simple ones – all of these are suitable. When you really start working with your own pressure cooker, you will make your own discoveries about the numerous things these wonderful vessels can achieve.

a sad omission

There is one type of food for which the pressure cooker just isn't suitable, and that is fish. See page 32 for further words of wisdom on the subject.

cleaning up

There's no rocket science in cleaning a pressure cooker, but you do have to keep the rubber gasket away from the dishwasher – so do the washing by hand. Some instruction manuals may say that the lid itself is dishwasher-safe, but I think washing by hand is better. When you put the gasket back in after washing, make sure it's fitted in place all over or the pressure cooker won't build up full pressure.

soups, sauces and relishes

If you used your pressure cooker for no other purpose than to cook soup, you wouldn't be wasting your money. The two were just made for each other. Soups that would take thirty minutes or more in an ordinary pan cook in as little as five minutes, and the meaty things that give so much flavour need under thirty minutes as compared to hours without pressure. The recipes here are just a few of my favourites. Once you've got the hang of your pressure cooker, you should start to experiment with adapting your own. What applies to soups applies equally to sauces, whose cooking times are radically cut under pressure. And the pressure cooker is also a very speedy way of making 'little' sauces, such as the three relishes here. Luncheon is served.

This old favourite is one of the most reliable soups about, as it makes use of one of the home cook's greatest allies: a bag of frozen peas. You should always have at least one bag of this excellent product in your freezer. The soup is ready in minutes. For an extra bit of luxury, fry some croutons to float on the soup.

minted pea soup

serves 4–6

1 small potato (about 100g), cut into pieces about 1.25cm thick
500g frozen peas
1 litre chicken or vegetable stock
50g butter
4 tablespoons double cream
8–10 fresh mint sprigs, finely chopped
salt and freshly ground black pepper

Put all the ingredients except half the mint sprigs and the cream in the pressure cooker. Clamp on the lid. Bring up to full pressure, turn the heat down to medium and cook for 10 minutes. Turn off the heat and leave to vent gradually.

Purée the vegetables using a blender or food processor. Return to the pressure cooker and keep hot until you need it, or leave to cool and reheat as necessary. Serve with a swirl of cream, a few grinds of pepper and the remaining mint on top.

This isn't really gazpacho, of course, but it brings in some extra complexity of flavour because of the thorough cooking (in all of five minutes) of the tomatoes and peppers. A great summertime treat.

cooked gazpacho

serves 4

1kg ripe, red tomatoes, halved, cores cut out
1kg red peppers, de-seeded and halved
1 onion, finely chopped
1 plump garlic clove, finely chopped
1 small red onion, finely chopped
1 tablespoon sherry vinegar
about 2 tablespoons extra virgin olive oil
½ large cucumber, de-seeded and cut into tiny dice
small handful fresh coriander, finely chopped
salt and freshly ground black pepper
fried croutons, to serve (optional)

Put the tomatoes, peppers, onion and garlic in the pressure cooker with 100ml water. Season with salt and plenty of freshly ground black pepper. Clamp on the lid. Bring up to full pressure, turn the heat down to medium and cook for 5 minutes. Turn off the heat and vent immediately.

Purée the mixture in a blender or food processor until smooth. Put a fine sieve over a serving bowl and strain the liquid in, pressing hard to extract all the juice. Chill the bowl for at least 4 hours, or put it in the freezer to speed things up.

In the meantime, put the chopped red onion in a small bowl with the sherry vinegar and leave to soak for at least 30 minutes; this softens the attack of the onion.

When the soup is well chilled and you're ready to serve, stir the onion and vinegar mixture into the soup with the olive oil. Taste for salt and pepper – it may need quite a bit more. Sprinkle on the cucumber dice and the coriander, and serve immediately. If you like, you can add some croutons of white bread fried in olive oil.

Note: this can be made with 2 x 400g tinned tomatoes if you can't get good fresh ones. And to alter the colour scheme, use yellow tomatoes and peppers.

Use the trimmed green parts from the leeks to make stock.

leek and potato soup

serves 4

3–4 medium leeks, white parts only, cut into pieces around 1.25cm thick
1 large baking potato (about 250g), cut into pieces around 1.25cm thick
750ml chicken stock or water
5–6 tablespoons double cream
chopped fresh parsley, chervil or chives, to garnish
salt and freshly ground black pepper

Put all the ingredients except the cream in the pressure cooker. Season with salt and freshly ground black pepper. Clamp on the lid. Bring up to full pressure, turn the heat down to medium and cook for 10 minutes. Turn off the heat and leave to vent gradually.

Purée the vegetables using a blender or food processor. Return to the pressure cooker and keep hot until you need it, or leave to cool and reheat as necessary. Serve with a swirl of cream and the herbs on top.

Note: you can increase the quantity of liquid to a maximum of 1 litre; this will make a thinner soup but will feed more people.

This can be adapted using other vegetables and beans.

a simple minestrone

serves 4–6

2 carrots (250g total weight), cut into 2.5cm chunks
2 potatoes (250g total weight), cut into 2.5cm chunks
3 celery sticks, cut into 2.5cm chunks
4 plump garlic cloves, roughly chopped
½ teaspoon each dried sage and oregano
1 litre chicken or vegetable stock
250g French beans, cut into 2.5cm lengths
400g can cannellini beans, rinsed and drained
small handful of fresh basil, chopped
3 tablespoons extra virgin olive oil
freshly grated Parmesan, to serve
salt and freshly ground black pepper

Put the carrots, potatoes, celery, garlic, sage, oregano and stock in the pressure cooker. Season with salt and freshly ground black pepper. Clamp on the lid. Bring up to full pressure, turn the heat down to medium and cook for 3 minutes. Turn off the heat and vent immediately. Add the two types of bean. Bring back to full pressure and cook for one minute more. Stir in the basil and oil when you are ready to serve, and pass the cheese round separately.

If you don't have sorrel, substitute 100g spinach and add the juice of half a lime just before serving. Use any combination of stock and milk that suits you for thinning out. Serve hot or cold.

sorrel, courgette and cucumber soup

serves 4

½ large cucumber, peeled, de-seeded and cut into fine dice
a good knob of butter
100g sorrel leaves, shredded
3 courgettes, thickly sliced
4 spring onions, roughly chopped
400g floury potatoes, peeled and cut into small chunks
600ml good chicken stock
150–200ml milk and/or stock for thinning
soured cream, to garnish
chopped chives, to garnish
salt and freshly ground black pepper

Put the cucumber in a colander and toss well with about 2 teaspoons of salt; leave for at least 30 minutes, then rinse and pat dry with kitchen paper.

Put the butter in the pressure cooker and add all remaining ingredients, except the milk or stock for thinning. Season well with salt and freshly ground black pepper. Clamp on the lid. Bring up to full pressure, turn down the heat to medium and cook for 5 minutes. Turn off the heat and vent immediately.

Purée the soup using a blender or food processor. If you're serving it cold, let it cool and then chill until needed. If you're eating it hot, tip it back into the pressure cooker and reheat gently. To finish, stir in the milk or extra stock (using more or less depending on how thick a soup you want). Serve with the cucumber dice sprinkled on top, plus a dollop of soured cream and, finally, chives.

This is a store-cupboard soup, highly versatile. You can get it cooking the instant you get home from work, and then either eat it straightaway or leave it sitting in the pressure cooker, if that suits your schedule. Note the procedure for cooking this soup for a larger crowd.

speedy bean soup

serves 1–2

1–2 bacon rashers, rinds removed and cut into shreds

400g can of beans – flageolets, cannellini, black-eyed, whatever

1 celery stick, coarsely chopped

1 carrot, coarsely chopped

1 plump garlic clove, finely chopped

1 small onion (about 100g), finely chopped

¼ teaspoon dried herbs – your choice

½ teaspoon mild chilli sauce or a few slices of fresh chilli, finely chopped

750ml chicken stock, fresh if possible

chopped fresh parsley, to garnish

Heat up at least 5cm water in your pressure cooker with the steamer insert (or an improvised steamer rack) in place. In the meantime, prepare all the ingredients. Put the bacon in a small non-stick frying pan and cook for 3–4 minutes, just long enough to brown it lightly.

Put all the ingredients into a heatproof bowl that will fit into your steamer with at least 2.5cm of space between the dish and side of the pan. Clamp on the lid. Bring up to full pressure, turn the heat down to medium and cook for 5 minutes. Turn off the heat and vent immediately. Eat straight away, garnished with parsley, or turn off the heat and leave to vent gradually and eat when you are ready. The soup will stay hot for a good 20 minutes. If you wish, you can mash some of the beans and stir them back into the soup to thicken it.

To cook this for a larger crowd, simply multiply the ingredients by two or three (three is the safe maximum) and brown the bacon in the pressure cooker itself. Put in all the remaining ingredients without using the steamer or bowl and cook for 5 minutes.

Note: grated cheese makes an excellent addition to this soup, sprinkled on lightly (or generously) at the table.

Ham hocks are often sold at very low prices and they pack a hefty wallop of flavour, capable of seasoning a big bucket of soup. This hearty soup makes a sustaining winter lunch served with crusty bread. It can also be made with the scrappy end from a boneless ham (generous butchers sell these for a song) or with a hunk of pancetta.

cabbage soup with ham hock

serves 4–6

1 ham hock (about 150–250g)
1 large white cabbage, sliced
2 large carrots, cut into thick chunks
2 onions, cut into thick chunks
4 garlic cloves, coarsely chopped
2 celery sticks, cut into thick chunks
2 small potatoes, peeled and cut into thick chunks

Put the hock in the pressure cooker with 1 litre water. Clamp on the lid. Bring up to full pressure, turn the heat down to medium and cook for 10 minutes. Turn off the heat and vent immediately.

Add the remaining ingredients to the pressure cooker. Clamp on the lid. Bring up to full pressure, turn the heat down to medium and cook for 10 minutes more. Turn off the heat and vent immediately or gradually, whichever suits your schedule. Remove the meat from the hambone, tear or cut it into small pieces, and return to the soup for serving.

A meal from bones: you can't get much cheaper, or tastier. Neck bones are most easily obtained from a butcher, who may even give them to you free of charge if you make friends with them.

lamb and barley soup

serves 4–6

1kg lamb bones, from the
　neck if possible
150g pearl barley
1 teaspoon herbes de
　Provence or similar
　herb mixture
4 plump garlic cloves
1.5 litres water, chicken
　or vegetable stock
3–4 celery sticks, sliced
　diagonally into 1.25cm
　pieces
3–4 large carrots, sliced
　diagonally into 1.25cm
　pieces
small handful of fresh
　flat-leaf parsley
salt and freshly ground
　black pepper

Put the bones, barley, herbs, garlic and stock in the pressure cooker. Clamp on the lid. Bring up to full pressure, turn the heat down to medium and cook for 25 minutes. Turn off the heat and vent immediately. Add the vegetables. Clamp on the lid. Bring up to full pressure, turn the heat down to medium and cook for another 2 minutes. Turn off the heat and vent immediately.

The liquid now needs to be degreased, which you can do most easily in one of three ways. One: let the soup settle and skim off the fat using a ladle or a long-handled, deep-bowled spoon. Two: use a dual-pour gravy boat. Three: let the soup cool and chill overnight (or until the fat has solidified). Break off the fat in pieces and discard – into the rubbish bin, not down the drain.

Reheat to serve, adjust the seasoning, and stir in the parsley.

Note: if you want to make the soup easier for your eaters to handle, you can pick the meat off the bones. Discard the bones and return the meat to the pan. For an informal weekend meal en famille, you can leave the bones in.

The pressure cooker makes a great tomato sauce, with or without meat, in little more time than it takes to boil water and cook pasta. The only trick here: keep the mince in large pieces, about the size of a golf ball, as large pieces will work better under pressure. This is a large quantity, too much for a single meal unless you are feeding a really large crowd. But you should make too much – you can freeze the rest and use it for a hassle-free meal some other night. There is enough here to sauce about 1.5kg of pasta.

ragù, after a fashion

serves 8–10

1–2 tablespoons
  vegetable oil
1kg lean minced beef
1 medium or 2 small
  onions (about 250g
  total weight)
6 plump garlic cloves,
  crushed
4 × 400g cans chopped
  tomatoes
2 tablespoons tomato
  purée
2 teaspoons dried mixed
  herbs, such as herbes
  de Provence
4 tablespoons red wine
50g butter
extra virgin olive oil, to
  taste
salt and freshly ground
  black pepper

Pour in enough vegetable oil to generously film the base of the pressure cooker. Heat to medium-hot, then add the mince and break it up into large chunks. Fry, stirring regularly, for 5–6 minutes or just long enough to brown most of the meat lightly. Now add the onions and garlic, and cook for 2–3 minutes or just long enough to make them smell really good.

Add all the remaining ingredients except the butter and olive oil, and season well with salt and freshly ground black pepper. Clamp on the lid. Bring up to full pressure, turn the heat down to medium and cook for 10 minutes. Turn off the heat and vent immediately. Take off the lid, turn the heat back on and add the butter. Let the sauce simmer for 5–10 minutes to reduce it slightly.

When you've sauced the pasta, add as much olive oil as you like. For each 500g of pasta, you will need about 3–4 tablespoons oil.

A classic of French bourgeois cooking, and so richly and deliciously simple it will win over even those who think they don't like cauliflower. This is heavily adapted from the recipe in *Michael Field's Cooking School*.

potage du barry

serves 8

50g butter
3 tablespoons plain flour
1 large or 2 small
   cauliflowers, trimmed
   and cut into florets
900ml chicken stock
3 egg yolks
125ml single cream
juice of ½ lemon
10–12 chives, finely
   chopped, to garnish
salt and freshly ground
   black or white pepper

Put the butter and flour in the pressure cooker. Melt the butter over a low heat, stirring the flour in constantly, just long enough to amalgamate the flour into the butter.

Add the cauliflower and stock to the pan and heat it up. Season with salt and freshly ground black pepper – or white pepper, for looks, if you happen to have some. Clamp on the lid. Bring up to full pressure, turn the heat down to medium and cook for 3 minutes. Turn off the heat and vent immediately.

While the soup is cooking, beat the egg yolks with the cream. When the pressure is low enough, take the lid off. Remove 8 nice-looking florets to use as a garnish. Purée the remaining soup, using a blender or food processor.

Reheat the soup gently, just to a simmer. Add the egg and cream mixture, a spoonful at a time, stirring constantly. When it is blended in and the soup is hot, serve immediately with a floret in each bowl and a sprinkling of chives on top.

This stuff can be unbearably hot if you use the fieriest chillies. Milder ones may work much better if you're not a chilli-fiend, so taste them before you buy. You have been warned. This is a good all-purpose relish, suitable for any meat or poultry dish, but also great with cold meats and cheese.

chilli relish

serves 4–6

150g green chillies, de-seeded if you wish, thinly sliced
2 small green peppers, de-seeded and sliced
1 small onion (about 100g), roughly chopped
4 plump garlic cloves, thinly sliced
½ teaspoon each cumin powder, coriander seeds and black mustard seeds
2 green cardamom pods
1 teaspoon salt
2 tablespoons vegetable oil
salt and freshly ground black pepper

Heat up at least 5cm water in your pressure cooker with the steamer insert (or an improvised steamer rack) in place. Put all the ingredients in a heatproof bowl that will fit in your pressure cooker with at least 2.5cm of space between the bowl and the side of the pan. Stir well, and season with salt and freshly ground black pepper. Clamp on the lid. Bring up to full pressure, turn the heat down to medium and cook for 5 minutes to keep a bit of crunch, 7–8 minutes if you want the vegetables softer.

This will keep well for up to a week in the fridge.

I made this to go with barbecued burgers, but its big flavours would go well with any simply-cooked red meat.

tomato and caper relish

serves 4–6

500g ripe cherry
    tomatoes, halved or
    quartered
2 plump garlic cloves,
    finely chopped
½ red chilli, finely
    chopped (optional)
½ teaspoon dried
    oregano
1 tablespoon vegetable oil
1 tablespoon tomato
    ketchup
2 teaspoons capers,
    roughly chopped
salt and freshly ground
    black pepper

Heat up at least 5cm water in your pressure cooker with the steamer insert (or an improvised steamer rack) in place. Put the tomatoes, garlic, chilli (if using), oregano, oil, ketchup, and half the capers in a heatproof dish that will fit in your steamer with at least 2.5cm of space between the dish and the side of the pan. Stir well, and season with salt and freshly ground black pepper. Clamp on the lid. Bring up to full pressure, turn the heat down to medium and cook for 5 minutes to keep a bit of crunch, 7–8 minutes if you want them softer. Turn off the heat and vent immediately.

When you can remove the lid, take out the bowl and stir in the remaining capers. Serve at room temperature, not fridge-cold.

This will keep well for up to a week in the fridge.

A zingy and appealing partner for fish and chicken. Or use as
a topping for grilled or barbecued vegetables. If you don't have
fresh herbs, use ½ teaspoon of dried.

courgette relish with lime

serves 4–6

2 plump garlic cloves,
  finely chopped
1 shallot, finely chopped
500g small courgettes,
  de-seeded and chopped
1 fresh thyme or
  tarragon sprig, leaves
  finely chopped
juice and grated zest of
  1 lime, plus extra juice
  if needed
2 tablespoons extra
  virgin olive oil
salt and freshly ground
  black pepper

Heat up at least 5cm water in your pressure cooker with
the steamer insert (or an improvised steamer rack) in
place. Put all the ingredients, except the olive oil, in a
heatproof bowl that will fit into your pressure cooker with
at least 2.5cm of space between the bowl and the side of
the pan. Stir well, and season with salt and freshly ground
black pepper. Clamp on the lid. Bring up to full pressure,
turn the heat down to medium and cook for 5 minutes to
keep a bit of crunch, 7–8 minutes if you want them softer.
Turn off the heat and vent immediately.

When the relish is cooked, leave it to cool, and then
add the oil. Taste for lime; if you want more of the fresh-
lime taste, add another teaspoon or so. Serve at room
temperature, not fridge-cold.

This will keep well for 3–4 days in the fridge.

fish in the pressure cooker

Fish is the least suited of all the major food groups to cooking in the pressure cooker. It isn't that you *can't* do it, it's just that there isn't much point – and for two reasons. One: fish cooks very quickly anyway, so the speed advantage conferred by pressure doesn't mean much here. Two: fish is usually a lean and fairly delicate form of animal protein, and it can go from perfect to overdone in the time it takes to read this paragraph – even if you read very fast. That predisposition requires watchfulness, and one thing you can't really do with a pressure cooker is watch the food as it cooks.

This is not to say that the pressure cooker can't come into contact with any food that began its existence in water. Two types of fishy dish do react well to pressure, and the first is larger cephalopods – octopus, cuttlefish or large squid suitable for stewing. These cook much faster in the pressure cooker than in conventional pans – about fifteen minutes as opposed to forty minutes, an hour, or even longer. Cook them in large pieces in water seasoned with garlic, a bay leaf and parsley, then add them to whatever sauce you feel like having.

The other important group of dishes is fish stew – or fish soup, if you just add a little more liquid. Here the vegetable base needs relatively short cooking, and the fish can be added at the end for gentle simmering.

fish stock

Making fish stock, by contrast to poultry or meat stock, never takes very long. The cooking time is measured in minutes rather than hours. But if you are making a fish stew like the one here, and you buy fish on the bone, you should use the discards for stock. Cloudiness won't matter so much because the stew itself is pretty murky stuff. So, wash the bones well (head included) to remove any traces of blood. Put them in the pressure cooker with a garlic clove, a small onion (halved), a bay leaf and a bouquet garni; if the bouquet is not homemade, include also a small handful of fresh parsley. Cover the mixture with water, as long as you don't fill the pressure cooker more than two-thirds full. Clamp on the lid. Bring up to full pressure, turn the heat down to medium, and cook for 5 minutes. Turn the heat off and leave to vent gradually. Strain the result well, but resign yourself to a cloudier stock than you would get if you cooked it conventionally.

Here is a sample recipe utilising the principle: a fish stew with vaguely Mediterranean origins. If you have a favourite fish stew, you can adapt it following my guidelines.

fish stew with saffron-chilli butter

serves 3–4

2 small carrots (about 200g), cut into 2.5cm chunks
1 small potato (about 100g), coarsely chopped
3 celery sticks, cut into 2.5cm chunks
200g French beans, cut into 2.5cm lengths
4 plump garlic cloves, roughly chopped
½ teaspoon each dried sage and oregano
750ml water, fish stock or vegetable stock
650g fish in boneless chunks
small handful of fresh parsley, coarsely chopped, to garnish

For the butter:
75g butter, softened
1 small red chilli, de-seeded and finely chopped
large pinch of saffron threads, crumbled
salt and freshly ground black pepper

First make the butter, at least two hours in advance. Put the butter in a bowl and season well with salt and freshly ground black pepper. Mix in the chilli and saffron, and mash until the solid ingredients are completely mixed in. Cover and chill.

Put the carrots, potato, celery, beans, garlic, sage, oregano and water or stock into the pressure cooker. Season with salt and freshly ground black pepper. Clamp on the lid, bring up to full pressure, turn the heat down to medium and cook for 3 minutes. Turn off the heat and vent immediately. Add the fish and the seasoned butter, then turn the heat back on and cook, without pressure, for 4–5 minutes, or until the fish is barely cooked. Sprinkle with the parsley and serve immediately.

meat

The pressure cooker is one of the best tools ever invented for cooking beef, pork and lamb. On its own it will not produce meat with a browned, crisp crust, but that's a small drawback given the numerous virtues. Its obvious benefits come in dishes that you would normally braise or stew or pot-roast. These delicious things take hours when cooked conventionally, but as little as twenty five minutes in the pressure cooker. It is now possible to make a stew – even from the toughest cuts – after getting home from work. And with minimal active work. But the pressure cooker does other things with meat. It cooks joints or chunks à point in flavourful liquid while preparing them for a final crisping in a frying pan. It poaches. It makes meaty soups, and cooks quickly and gently for use in sandwiches or salads. And there are probably dozens of other things that I haven't even discovered yet. I look forward to making their acquaintance.

This is my basic braise, because it is laughably quick and easy. You can cook vegetables for serving with a few minutes of extra work, but if you're lazy or pressed for time (or both), you can just cook the beef in the pressure cooker and prepare a side dish separately.

my basic pressure-braised beef

serves 2

2–3 tablespoons vegetable oil
600g braising beef in four pieces
1 garlic bulb, cloves separated but unpeeled
2 carrots, quartered
2 celery sticks, quartered
250g smallish potatoes, unpeeled and halved
2 teaspoons flour
2 teaspoons brandy
400g can chopped tomatoes
2 teaspoons red wine vinegar
1 teaspoon mixed herbs, such as herbes de Provence
450ml red wine
salt and freshly ground black pepper

Pour in enough vegetable oil to generously film the base of the pressure cooker, and heat to medium-high. Brown the beef all over, for just a couple of minutes per side, to get some colour into it. You will have to do this in at least two batches.

Pour off the excess oil from the pan and turn the heat down to low. Add 1 tablespoon fresh oil. Add the garlic, carrot, celery and potatoes. Stir briskly, scraping the base of the pan to dislodge the browning residue, then add the flour and stir well until it begins to take on a little colour. Stir in the brandy and let it sizzle for a moment. Put the beef back in, turn the heat up to high, and dump in the tomatoes, vinegar, herbs, wine and seasoning.

Clamp on the lid. Bring up to full pressure, turn the heat down to medium, and cook for 25 minutes. Turn off the heat and let the steam vent gradually.

The braising liquid can be reduced if you wish, in order to concentrate its flavour. Remove all the solid ingredients and simmer the liquid briskly for 5 minutes or so, then return the meat and vegetables to the pan and reheat quickly.

Note: the carrot and celery shouldn't be served, as they are included to give flavour and will have cooked to extreme mushiness. If you want to have edible vegetables in the stew, cut up an extra pair of celery sticks and carrots. Cook the beef and vegetables for 25 minutes. Turn off the heat and vent immediately. Put the additional celery and carrots in. Clamp on the lid. Bring up to full pressure, turn the heat down to medium, and cook for 5 minutes. Discard the long-cooked vegetables before serving.

This is a perfect summertime dish when dinner guests are coming but you don't have much time to cook. Serve with a salsa verde (see page 77) and everyone will be happy. This will feed six people and leave plenty of leftovers.

poached beef with vegetables

serves 6

1 joint of aitch-bone or topside (about 1.5kg)
1.5 litres water
1–2 vegetable stock cubes, preferably Just Bouillon
2 plump garlic cloves
5 black peppercorns
a bouquet garni or 1 teaspoon dried mixed herbs
200g leek or onion, halved
2 celery sticks, halved
2 carrots, halved
small handful of fresh parsley, stalks included
about 1.5kg mixed vegetables, such as celery, fennel, young leeks, young carrots, new potatoes, cut into bite-sized pieces
salt and freshly ground black pepper
salsa verde, capers or mustard, to serve

Put all the ingredients except the mixed vegetables in the pressure cooker. Clamp on the lid. Bring up to full pressure, turn the heat down to medium and cook for 30 minutes. Turn off the heat and vent immediately. As soon as you can open the lid, remove everything and discard the vegetables. Put the liquid through a fine sieve and return to the pressure cooker.

Add the mixed vegetables to the pressure cooker. Season with salt and freshly ground black pepper. Clamp on the lid. Bring up to full pressure, turn the heat down to medium and cook for 5 minutes. Slice the beef 1.25cm thick and arrange it on a platter with the vegetables surrounding it. Serve with a good assortment of condiments: salsa verde, capers, mustard, and so on – or just serve good mustard.

This is adapted from a recipe in Jane Grigson's *Charcuterie and French Pork Cookery*, one of the indispensable works for committed omnivores. Being fairly rich, it is a good party dish. And like all dishes of the kind, it is, in Grigson's words, 'better made one day and heated through the next'.

jarret de boeuf en daube

serves 8

750g pork belly, cut into large bite-sized pieces
750g shin of beef, cut into large bite-sized pieces
plain flour, seasoned with salt and freshly ground black pepper
2–3 tablespoons vegetable oil for browning
3 large onions, thickly sliced
300ml good stock
300ml red wine
3 juniper berries, bruised
1 bay leaf
2 plump garlic cloves, finely chopped
1 teaspoon dried thyme
1 teaspoon dried rosemary

Roll the meat in the seasoned flour and shake off the excess. Film the base of the pressure cooker with 1–2 tablespoons vegetable oil and heat it to medium-hot. Brown the pieces all over, just for a couple of minutes per side, to get some colour into them. Repeat with the remaining meat until it's all browned.

Pour off the excess oil from the pan and turn the heat down to low. Put in 1 tablespoon fresh oil. Brown the onions lightly, with regular stirring. Pour in a little water and scrape the base of the pan thoroughly to release the flavourful stuck-on bits, then pour in the stock and the wine. Get the pan bubbling while you put in the meat and then the seasonings.

Clamp on the lid. Bring up to full pressure, turn the heat down to medium and cook for 25 minutes. Turn off the heat and vent immediately. Test the two meats by sticking a fork in – it should go in easily, and the meat should be meltingly soft. If necessary, cook for another 5 minutes under pressure.

Serve immediately, if you must, but waiting a day is much better. Rice or potatoes and perhaps some braised cabbage (see page 117) are good partners.

This is one of the best ways I know of using this supremely flavourful and delightfully inexpensive cut of beef. My wife regards it as her favourite dish on earth – and I am inclined to agree with her. Ask your butcher to give you boneless slices, and consider buying a whole shin: it freezes well. Important: save the cooking liquid for soup.

shin of beef
with an asian dipping sauce

serves 4

about 750g shin of beef, cut into 2.5cm thick pieces
1 star anise
2.5cm hunk of fresh root ginger, peeled
1 plump garlic clove, peeled
small handful of fresh coriander, leaves only, to garnish

For the sauce:
6 tablespoons soy sauce
3 tablespoons red wine vinegar
1 teaspoon Thai fish sauce
1 tablespoon vegetable oil
1 teaspoon sesame oil
2 spring onions, finely sliced
1 plump garlic clove, finely chopped
1 small chilli, de-seeded if you wish, and finely chopped

Put the beef in the pressure cooker with 1 litre of water and the star anise, ginger and garlic. Clamp on the lid. Bring up to full pressure, turn the heat down to medium, and cook for 15 minutes. Turn off the heat and leave to vent gradually. In the meantime, make the sauce by mixing all the ingredients together in a serving bowl.

When you're ready to serve, take the beef out of the pressure cooker and cut or shred it into bite-sized pieces. Garnish with the coriander and serve with plain boiled rice and the sauce passed separately.

Note: you can also cook the beef for 20 minutes and vent immediately. If you do that, you can keep the beef warm in some of the cooking liquid and cook your rice in the pressure cooker (see page 96).

Final note: cutting the beef into slices shortens the cooking time. If you want to present the beef for slicing at the table, add 10–15 minutes to the cooking time.

This is a fairly straightforward but nicely complex meatloaf.

meatloaf for company

serves 6–8

750g lean minced beef or lamb
1 thick slice cooked ham, including all
  its fat, finely chopped
1 onion (about 150–200g), finely
  chopped
1 small courgette, finely chopped
1 small carrot, finely chopped
1 celery stick, finely chopped
250g cooked rice or fresh breadcrumbs
small handful of parsley, finely chopped
1 tablespoon dried mixed herbs, such
  as herbes de Provence
50g butter
2 eggs, lightly beaten
salt and freshly ground black pepper

Mix all the ingredients in a large bowl using your bare hands, and season well with salt and freshly ground black pepper. Heat up at least 5cm water in your pressure cooker with the steamer insert (or an improvised steamer rack) in place. Put the mixture in a soufflé dish, or something similar, which will fit into your pressure cooker with at least a 2.5cm gap between the dish and the side of the pan. Pack down firmly and place in the pressure cooker. Clamp on the lid. Bring up to full pressure, turn the heat down to medium, and cook for 25 minutes. Turn off the heat and leave to vent gradually. (You can brown the top of the loaf quickly under a hot grill, if you like.)

If serving hot, take care when slicing, because the texture will be slightly crumbly. If serving cold or at room temperature, put a plate with a heavy weight on top while the loaf is cooling, to firm up the texture.

Very tasty stuff. Add another chilli if you really crave the burn.

asian-flavoured meatloaf

serves 4

1 small onion (about 50g), finely
  chopped
2 thin slices fresh root ginger, peeled
  and finely chopped
1 small red chilli, de-seeded if you
  wish, finely chopped
1 plump garlic clove, finely chopped
1 tablespoon vegetable oil
2 teaspoons Thai fish sauce
2 teaspoons red wine vinegar
1 tablespoon soy sauce
small handful cooked rice or fresh
  breadcrumbs
small handful fresh coriander, finely
  chopped
450g lean minced pork, beef or lamb
  (or a combination)

Put the onion, ginger, chilli and garlic in a small pan, or microwave-suitable bowl, with the vegetable oil. Heat the pan gently on the hob, or put the bowl in the microwave, for a few minutes, just to soften everything lightly. Add the fish sauce, vinegar and soy sauce, and leave to cool.

Heat up at least 5cm water in your pressure cooker with the steamer insert (or an improvised steamer rack) in place. Mix all the ingredients in a medium heatproof dish that will fit into your steamer with at least 2.5cm of space between the dish and the side of the pan. Pack down firmly and place in the pressure cooker. Clamp on the lid. Bring up to full pressure, turn the heat down to medium, and cook for 15 minutes. Leave to vent gradually. (You can brown the top of the loaf quickly under a hot grill, if you like.)

Oxtail is the perfect cut of meat for the pressure cooker; tough but full of flavour, it is transformed to melt-in-the-mouth softness when cooked under pressure. If the meat is very fatty, trim off most of it – but leave a little to provide more succulence and flavour.

oxtail braised in beer

serves 4–6

about 2 tablespoons
vegetable oil
2kg oxtail, trimmed of fat
if necessary
1 large onion, sliced
3–4 garlic cloves,
unpeeled
1 bay leaf
1 teaspoon herbes de
Provence or similar
herb mixture
1 teaspoon plain flour
660ml bottle of beer,
anything except lager

Heat the vegetable oil in the pressure cooker or in a frying pan. Brown the oxtail, a few pieces at a time, trying to get some colour on all surfaces; don't despair if you can't brown them evenly. When they're all done, remove from the pan. Add a little more oil if needed and cook the onion briefly to get some colour into it – just a couple of minutes will do.

Put all the ingredients in the pressure cooker and clamp the lid on. Bring up to full pressure, turn the heat down to medium and cook for 25 minutes, then turn the heat off and let the steam vent gradually. As soon as you can remove the lid, test the beef for doneness by pulling off a bit and eating it. If it isn't meltingly soft, put it back in and cook for another 5 minutes. Serve with mashed potatoes to soak up the flavourful cooking liquid.

pork loin

Small joints of boneless pork loin are wonderful for pressure cooking. They cook fast, and they're versatile – good for two people and good for a larger crowd. That's why I've put in a few recipes for it – each one quite different – preceded by a recipe for cooking the pork itself. If you are cooking for more than two, simply double the quantities here.

Try to choose a fairly thin piece of loin, about 7.5cm in diameter at its thickest. If the piece is thicker, however, simply add a few extra minutes to the cooking time. Note: the weight is immaterial. A short piece and a long piece take the same time to cook as long as they are of the same thickness.

basic pork loin

serves 2

1 piece of boneless pork loin (about 7.5cm in diameter at its thickest)

Put the pork in the pressure cooker and pour in water to a depth of 5cm. Clamp on the lid. Bring up to full pressure, turn the heat down to medium and cook for 10 minutes. Turn off the heat and vent immediately.

If the pork is somewhat thicker, add 2–3 minutes to the cooking time, but don't be tempted to do it for too much longer than that. The pork will be dry if overcooked, as loin is a lean cut.

Marinating overnight in a dry marinade gives excellent flavour, but only if you have the rind removed first. Ask the butcher to do this for you before re-rolling, and ask also for just about 1cm of fat to be left on. If you're an enterprising sort, you will take the rind home and use it to make crackling.

marinated pork loin

serves 3–4

¼ teaspoon each dried thyme, rosemary and sage
½ teaspoon freshly ground black pepper
¼ teaspoon coarse salt
1 plump garlic clove, finely chopped
1 piece of boneless pork loin (about 7.5cm in diameter at its thickest and about 12.5–15cm long)
1–2 tablespoons vegetable oil

Mix all the ingredients together, except the oil, and rub them all over the pork, trying to distribute them as evenly as possible. Put the pork in a small glass or ceramic dish, cover it tightly, and chill for at least 8 hours or overnight. Remove from the fridge an hour before you plan to cook.

Heat up at least 5cm water in your pressure cooker with the steamer insert (or an improvised steamer rack) in place. Put the pork in a heatproof dish that will fit into your steamer with at least 2.5cm of space between the dish and the side of the pan. Put the dish in the pressure cooker and clamp on the lid. Bring up to full pressure, turn the heat down to medium and cook for 8 minutes. Turn off the heat and vent immediately. While the pork is cooking, get out a non-stick frying pan and add a little vegetable oil.

Heat the oil in the pan and fry the pork briskly, turning regularly, just long enough to complete the cooking and get a little colour into it. Any juices left in the steaming dish can be degreased and served with the pork.

*This recipe is shamelessly lifted from my book The Green
Kitchen. I reproduce it here because it is (he said immodestly)
a humdinger. A piece of boned and rolled loin is excellent used
this way, although shoulder of pork is the other top choice.*

pork loin, potatoes and crackling

serves 2–3

300g large new potatoes
2 small onions, sliced
2 carrots, sliced or cut
  into thick batons
300ml water or light
  stock
½ teaspoon herbes
  de Provence or dried
  thyme, rosemary or
  sage
350g piece of boned and
  rolled pork (about
  10cm long and 10cm
  thick)
1–2 tablespoons
  vegetable oil
salt and freshly ground
  black pepper

Put the potatoes in the pressure cooker, followed by the onions, carrots, liquid and herbs. Season with salt and plenty of pepper. There should be just enough stock to barely cover the vegetables. Put the pork on top. Clamp on the lid. Bring up to full pressure, turn the heat down to medium and cook for 10 minutes. Turn off the heat and vent immediately.

Film a large, heavy frying pan generously with oil; the pan must be large enough to accommodate the meat. Put it over a medium heat and cook the pork with the skin side down, turning it as each section of skin turns to crackling. To finish, brown the meaty surfaces lightly. The whole procedure should take no more than 10 minutes – which, added to the pressure cooking time, is far less than roasting the joint would take.

Serve with the potatoes and some of the cooking liquid as gravy.

Cook in the pressure cooker, brown in a pan.
Ready in little more than 30 minutes.

a speedy pork 'roast'

serves 4

800g rolled shoulder
  of pork
1–2 tablespoons
  vegetable oil
1 teaspoon dried mixed
  herbs, such as herbes
  de Provence
small handful of fresh
  parsley, finely chopped
salt and freshly ground
  black pepper

Heat up at least 5cm water in your pressure cooker with the steamer insert (or an improvised steamer rack) in place. Put the pork in a heatproof dish that will fit into your steamer with at least 2.5cm of space between the dish and the side of the pan. Put the dish in the pressure cooker and clamp on the lid. Bring up to full pressure, turn the heat down to medium and cook for 25 minutes. Turn off the heat and vent immediately.

While you're waiting for the lid to be ready to come off, film the base of a heavy frying pan with oil and heat it up to a moderate heat. When the pork comes out, season with salt and freshly ground black pepper, and dust with the mixed herbs. Brown the pork as thoroughly as you can, and try getting the skin to crackle during browning – sometimes this works, and sometimes it doesn't, but it is always worth a try.

While the pork is browning, degrease the liquid from the dish and season with salt and freshly ground black pepper. Mix in the parsley and serve with the pork.

This is dead easy, very quick and really tasty. If you want to serve more than four people, the recipe can easily be multiplied. Note: if you wish, you can add a red chilli, de-seeded and finely chopped, to the other salad ingredients. Extra note: if you can't find fresh lime leaves, buy the dry ones and soften them in a little warm water before shredding. Final note: if you wish, you can score lines in the cucumber skin; this gives an attractive visual effect, and the dressing gets into the ridges.

thai-style pork salad

serves 3–4

For the dressing:
3 tablespoons
  vegetable oil
1 teaspoon sesame
  oil
1 teaspoon Thai fish
  sauce
2 tablespoons soy
  sauce
juice of 2 limes
½ small chilli, de-
  seeded and finely
  chopped
1 thin slice fresh
  root ginger, finely
  chopped
1 small garlic clove,
  finely chopped or
  crushed
3–4 kaffir lime
  leaves, shredded

For the salad:
1 piece of boneless
  pork loin (about
  7.5cm in diameter
  at its thickest and
  600g in weight)
6–8 cos lettuce
  leaves, very thinly
  sliced
1 cucumber, de-
  seeded and thinly
  sliced
1 red pepper, de-
  seeded and thinly
  sliced
3 celery sticks,
  thinly sliced
  diagonally
3 spring onions,
  thinly sliced
  diagonally
small handful of
  coriander or
  holy basil leaves,
  finely chopped,
  to garnish

Mix the dressing ingredients at least 1 hour in advance of cooking so that the flavours will have time to blend.

Cook the pork as for Basic Pork Loin on page 46. When it's done, leave to rest for at least 15 minutes before slicing. In the meantime, prepare all the salad ingredients and put into a serving bowl. Slice the pork as thinly as you can manage and lay it on top of the salad. Stir the dressing quickly, pour it over and toss. Garnish with the coriander or basil, and serve immediately.

These cheap, tasty and eminently satisfying bones are perfect in the pressure cooker and can be transformed into other dishes with minimal effort. Here is a trio of dishes, each feeding two people. After you have made the trio of knuckles on the first day, you can chill the remainder for five days or freeze them, rubbed with a little vegetable oil and tightly sealed. Needless to say, if you prefer, you can serve all three knuckles to six hungry eaters in any one of the incarnations.

pork knuckles:
three dishes for two people

dish one:
braised knuckles with red chilli salsa

serves 2

3 large pork knuckles, from leg or shoulder (about 2kg total weight)
2–3 plump garlic cloves
1 small onion, peeled but left whole
rice or potatoes, to serve

For the salsa:
1 small red chilli, finely chopped
1 small red onion, finely chopped
large pinch of ground coriander and cumin

Put the knuckles in the pressure cooker with the garlic and onion, and fill the pan with water to come about one third of the way up. Clamp on the lid. Bring up to full pressure, turn the heat down to medium and cook for 30 minutes. Turn off the heat and let the steam vent gradually, then pull out one of the knuckles. Meanwhile, mix the salsa ingredients together in a bowl.

Slice the meat off the bone and serve with the salsa, moistened with a spoonful of the braising liquid, and some plain boiled rice or potatoes. Reserve the braising liquid in two batches with the remaining knuckles to use with the other recipes.

dish two:
braised knuckle with potatoes, carrots and garlic

serves 2

1 cooked knuckle
1 potato, peeled and cut in thick chunks
2 large carrots, peeled and cut in thick chunks
1 garlic bulb, separated and peeled
1 small strip of lemon zest
braising liquid and stock or water as required
salt and freshly ground black pepper
small handful of chopped parsley, to garnish

Combine all the ingredients in the pressure cooker, adding liquid to come up about one third of the way, and season with salt and freshly ground black pepper. Clamp on the lid. Bring up to full pressure, turn the heat down to medium and cook for 5 minutes. Turn off the heat and vent the steam immediately, then cut the meat off the bone. Serve with the vegetables, garlic and a little of the braising liquid plus a small handful of chopped parsley sprinkled on top.

dish three:
knuckle soup with rice and celery

serves 2

125ml white long grain rice
1 cooked knuckle
4 celery sticks, thinly sliced
1 slice fresh root ginger, peeled and finely chopped
1 tablespoon tomato ketchup
5ml Worcestershire sauce
15ml soy sauce
braising liquid and stock or water as required

Wash the rice by soaking it in cold water for a few minutes, then drain and rinse, and repeat the process one more time; this is useful for getting rid of the excess starch.

Put all the ingredients in the pressure cooker, adding liquid to come up about one third of the way. Clamp on the lid. Bring up to full pressure, turn the heat down to medium and cook for 5 minutes. Turn off the heat and vent immediately. Cut the meat off the bone, and serve with the remaining liquid. A side salad completes the meal.

This classic of Chinese home cooking couldn't be simpler in the pressure cooker. Easy enough for a midweek dinner, it needs nothing more than boiled rice and a green vegetable.

red-cooked pork

serves 3–4

600g thick piece of
  boneless pork, from
  shoulder, leg or belly
100ml soy sauce
400ml water
1 star anise
½ teaspoon Sichuan
  peppercorns
3 plump garlic cloves,
  peeled
1 thick slice of fresh root
  ginger, peeled

Put all the ingredients in the pressure cooker. Clamp on the lid. Bring up to full pressure, turn the heat down to medium and cook for 30 minutes. Turn the heat off and leave to vent gradually. Serve with plain boiled rice and some stir-fried vegetables, and with extra soy sauce and some chilli sauce if you wish. The cooking liquid is fairly salty and should be served in moderation. Economical cooks freeze it and use it for another pot of pork – but it does take up quite a lot of freezer space.

Potée is a French dish comprising a hearty soup in which fairly large pieces of meat and vegetables are simmered together for a long time. The pieces are then cut up for serving. Many of the French regions have their own version, which may include just about any red meat you care to name – and sometimes poultry as well. My version is loosely modelled on the one in *French Country Cooking* by Albert and Michel Roux. Use whatever meats you like, but use at least three types, including something cured or smoked, and make sure all the vegetables get in there – they're vital for the complexity of the broth.

potée

serves 4–6

250g fairly lean bacon or pancetta, in a single piece
500g boned and rolled shoulder of pork
1 small white cabbage, quartered
300g new potatoes, halved
250g small turnips, halved or quartered
250g small carrots, halved if necessary
250g small leeks, cut into 2.5cm lengths
3–4 small onions, halved or quartered
1 garlic bulb, cloves separated but unpeeled
1 bouquet garni
2 cloves
5 whole black peppercorns
500g cooking sausage such as kielbasa, pricked in a few places with a fork

Put the bacon in the pressure cooker with 7.5cm of water. Clamp on the lid. Bring up to full pressure, turn the heat down to medium and cook for 3 minutes. Vent the steam immediately, take out the bacon and discard the water.

Put the bacon back in the pressure cooker with the pork shoulder and fill it one-third full with water. Clamp on the lid. Bring up to full pressure, turn the heat down to medium and cook for 20 minutes. Vent the steam immediately and remove the meats, then add all the remaining ingredients to the pressure cooker. Clamp on the lid. Bring up to full pressure, turn the heat down to medium and cook for 5 minutes. Turn off the heat and vent immediately. Put the pork and bacon back in the pressure cooker for a couple of minutes, just to heat them up.

Put the meats and vegetables on a carving platter and slice into manageable pieces. Serve in shallow bowls, with the broth passed separately.

This can also be made with a chicken if you can't get or don't like rabbit.

braised rabbit with mustard and capers

serves 4

2 smallish rabbits (about
    750g each)
2 tablespoons vegetable
    oil
3 tablespoons flour
4 small onions (about
    75g total weight),
    peeled but left whole
400ml stock
400ml dry white wine
2 tablespoons grainy
    mustard
3–4 fresh tarragon or
    thyme sprigs, or 1
    teaspoon dried
2 teaspoons capers,
    coarsely chopped
2 teaspoons cornflour
    (optional)
salt and freshly ground
    black pepper
small handful of fresh
    parsley, finely chopped,
    to garnish

Joint the rabbits or have this done for you by the butcher. Soak them for 20 minutes in salted water to remove any traces of blood, then drain well. Heat the oil in the pressure cooker and brown the rabbit pieces quickly – don't worry about getting them uniformly brown. Season with a little salt and plenty of freshly ground black pepper. Add the flour and stir well with the rabbit. Put in the onions and toss with the rabbit, then pour in the stock, wine, mustard and herbs. Finally, put in half the capers. Clamp on the lid. Bring up to full pressure, turn the heat down to medium and cook for 30 minutes. Turn off the heat and vent the steam immediately. As soon as you can take off the lid, put in the remaining capers.

If the cooking liquid is not thick enough for your taste, you can thicken it up by reducing it over a moderate heat for a few minutes or by whisking in the cornflour with a spoonful of the cooking liquid. Blend well and stir into the liquid in the pan.

When you're ready to eat, put the rabbit pieces in a bowl and pour over the liquid. Garnish with the parsley and serve immediately with boiled rice or potatoes.

The model here is a French dish called *gigot à sept heures*, leg of lamb cooked for seven hours. My version uses shoulder instead of leg, and obviously takes a lot less time than seven hours. The meat ends up soft enough to be cut with a spoon. Note: this recipe calls for stuffing the shoulder before it is rolled. You can do this yourself if you're handy with kitchen twine, but you'll do better to prepare the stuffing at home and take it to the butcher so that he can do the rolling. He's better at it. You can start preparations the night before, if you like.

seven-hour shoulder of lamb
(in 40 minutes)

serves 4–6

1 boned shoulder of lamb
  (about 1.5kg)
400ml dry white wine
3–4 leeks, cut into
  1.25cm slices
1–2 tablespoons
  vegetable oil

For the stuffing:
3–4 plump garlic cloves
small handful of fresh
  parsley, finely chopped
1 teaspoon dried
  rosemary, crumbled
1 teaspoon fine salt
freshly ground black
  pepper

Get the butcher to remove the shank (save it for another meal) and bone the shoulder. Mix all the stuffing ingredients and spread them out on the inside of the meat. Tie the shoulder securely. At this point you can, if you wish, leave the shoulder in the fridge overnight; some of the flavour from the stuffing will get into the meat.

Put the lamb in the pressure cooker with the wine, and clamp on the lid. Bring up to full pressure, turn the heat down to medium and cook for 35 minutes. Turn off the heat and vent immediately. Put the leeks in the pan. Bring up to full pressure, turn the heat down to medium and cook for 5 minutes more. Turn off the heat and vent immediately.

To finish the dish, lift the lamb out of its liquid and drain well. Heat a large frying pan with just enough oil to coat the base in a thin film. Brown the lamb on all surfaces, or as thoroughly as you can. In the meantime, boil the cooking liquid to reduce it somewhat and concentrate its flavour. Serve the cooking liquid as a gravy, with the leeks alongside, and simply cooked potatoes to accompany the meat.

This is a great way to have a seriously well-flavoured piece of lamb on the table in little more than thirty minutes. The braising cooks the meat until tender; the frying crisps it up; and the cooking liquid provides a tasty gravy. Get your butcher to cut the shoulder in half for you.

spicy braised and fried shoulder of lamb

serves 4–6

1 shoulder of lamb, shank removed, cut in half
225ml dry white wine
225ml chicken or vegetable stock
1–2 tablespoons vegetable oil
1 small chilli, de-seeded if you wish, finely chopped
½ teaspoon each of cumin, coriander and fennel seeds
3 plump garlic cloves, finely chopped
1 small onion, finely chopped
salt and freshly ground black pepper
small handful of fresh mint or coriander, finely chopped, to garnish

Put the lamb, wine and stock in the pressure cooker. Season with salt and freshly ground black pepper. Clamp on the lid. Bring up to full pressure, turn the heat down to medium and cook for 35 minutes. Turn off the heat and vent immediately. Remove the lamb as soon as you can open the lid, and in the meantime, heat a large non-stick frying pan with a little oil.

Put the lamb in the frying pan and brown well on both sides (about 5 minutes). While it's cooking, boil the cooking liquid in the pressure cooker at a moderate pace to reduce it in volume by about half. When the lamb is nearly ready, add the spices to the frying pan with the garlic and onion, and let them cook for a couple of minutes. Garnish with the herbs and pass the gravy around in a gravy boat.

The only thing I hate about lamb shanks is that they've gone from being an unloved cheapo cut (some butchers used to give them away) to one that's sought-after and therefore expensive. Oh well. I prefer shoulder shanks because they're (a) cheaper and (b) rich in collagen, which melts during long, slow cooking to produce a gelatinous texture. (Note that the pressure cooker replaces 'long, slow cooking' with very speedy cooking and gelatinises the collagen just as effectively.) Note also that leg shanks will work equally well, and that you can add your own choice of extra herbs and spices to the rub.

lamb shanks with a spanish-style spice rub

serves 4

4 lamb shanks, preferably shoulder shanks (each about 500–600g)
2 teaspoons pimentón or paprika
2 teaspoons dried oregano
2 teaspoons fine salt
6–8 plump garlic cloves, finely chopped or crushed
4 tablespoons vegetable oil
150ml dry white wine, sherry or water

Put the shanks in a heatproof dish that has a lid; if you don't have one with a lid, you can cover the dish with aluminium foil. Mix all the other ingredients except the wine in a small bowl and rub them all over the lamb pieces. Chill for at least 8 hours, and overnight if possible.

Put the shanks in the pressure cooker with the wine, sherry or water and clamp on the lid. Bring up to full pressure, turn the heat down to medium, and cook for 25 minutes if you want the meat to have a hint of bite to it, or 30 minutes if you like falling-off-the-bone softness. Turn off the heat and leave to vent gradually.

If you wish, you can get more colour into the lamb and some nice browning flavours, by flashing it quickly under a hot grill. You will need about 10 minutes, turning once. This intensely flavoursome dish needs some plain rice or mashed potato as an accompaniment.

A simple dish that's even better when reheated. If you want it hotter, add a whole small chilli such as the fiery Scotch bonnet. But remove before serving, unless there is a masochist at the table.

curried lamb

serves 6–8

1.5kg boneless lamb shoulder, cut into large chunks
about 3 tablespoons flour
2 tablespoons vegetable oil
4 large carrots, cut into 5cm lengths
1 large onion, cut into large chunks
4 garlic cloves, halved
1–2 tablespoons mild curry powder
400g can chopped tomatoes
wine and chicken stock as needed (700–800ml total liquid)
salt and freshly ground black pepper

Dust the lamb with flour, season with salt and pepper, and heat the oil to medium-hot in the pressure cooker. Brown the meat lightly, doing no more than two or three pieces at a time. Remove to a plate or bowl as they're done. Add the carrots, onion, garlic and curry powder to the pan. Stir for a minute, adding a little water to deglaze.

Return the meat to the pressure cooker and add the tomatoes, stock and wine; there should be just enough liquid to cover the meat, and try to use about half wine and half stock. Clamp on the lid. Bring up to full pressure, turn the heat down to medium and cook for 25 minutes. Vent immediately and check the meat; it should be soft, almost at falling-off-the-bone stage. Cook again for 5 more minutes if you think it needs it. Serve with mashed potatoes or plain rice.

poultry

I eat more poultry than any other form of animal protein, and more and more I find myself cooking it in the pressure cooker. With poultry as with meat, you can't get a browned, crisp skin from the pressure cooker alone. But crisp skin is not the only point of poultry. The pressure cooker turns out various dishes of real excellence, braises, stews, soups. In some cases you can brown the skin afterwards if you wish to, but I don't think it's necessary. The one thing that is *always* necessary with poultry is to buy the best you can afford. You can have the best chicken recipe in the world (from this book I would nominate Chicken with 40 Cloves of Garlic, page 80), but if you make it with cheap, crummy chicken that has soft flesh and less flavour than your average shoebox, you will be missing most of the point of the dish. I am also very enthusiastic about duck in the pressure cooker. Again, the skin doesn't crisp up, but melting softness throughout brings out a different dimension of the delectable ducky character. And do note the Five-Spice Duck (page 89), in which the skin is crisped up after pressure cooking. This is one of my favourite pressure cooker dishes, and a good one for dinner parties if you do the initial cooking a day in advance.

A vaguely Spanish dish, exploiting the affinity between chicken and sherry. If you like, you can put in a large handful of tiny button mushrooms when you add the olives; they will heat through to a sort of semi-cooked state during the resting time.

chicken with sherry, mustard and olives

serves 4

2–3 tablespoons
   vegetable oil
8 chicken thighs,
   or 4 breasts
4 onions, halved
2 teaspoons French
   mustard
100ml dry sherry
   mixed with 150ml
   water or chicken
   stock
1 tablespoon sherry
   vinegar (or red wine
   vinegar)
16 large green olives,
   plain or flavoured
   with herbs
large handful of
   parsley, coarsely
   chopped
salt and freshly
   ground black pepper

Pour some oil into the pressure cooker, using just enough to coat the base of the pan generously. Put in 4 thighs or 2 breasts and turn the heat to medium-high. Brown the pieces lightly, then remove to a plate and brown the remainder.

Put the pieces back in the pressure cooker and add the onions and mustard, stirring the pieces to distribute the mustard evenly. Season with salt and pepper, pour in the sherry mixture and vinegar, and clamp on the lid. Bring up to full pressure, turn the heat down to medium and cook for 10 minutes. Turn off the heat and vent the steam immediately.

As soon as you can take the lid off, put the olives in the pan and put the lid back on. Leave for 5 minutes, then stir in the parsley and serve with rice or mashed potatoes.

A one-pot meal for four people.

chicken with vegetables

serves 4

4 chicken pieces,
  breast or (better) leg,
  separated into thighs
  and drumsticks
2–3 tablespoons vegetable
  oil
4 small parsnips,
  unpeeled
4 small turnips, unpeeled
2 lemons, halved
½ teaspoon dried
  tarragon
½ teaspoon dried thyme
300ml liquid – chicken
  stock, dry white
  wine or water (or a
  combination)
salt and freshly ground
  black pepper
chopped fresh parsley, to
  garnish

Put the chicken pieces in the pan two at a time with some vegetable oil, and brown them very quickly. Take them out and put in the parsnips and turnips, then the lemon and the herbs. Put the chicken pieces on top and season with salt and pepper, then pour over the liquid. Clamp on the lid. Bring up to full pressure, turn the heat down to medium and cook for 10 minutes. Turn off the heat and vent immediately. Serve as soon as you can open the lid. Plain boiled rice makes a good accompaniment, and some chopped parsley on top adds a little colour.

This is a mangled version of the best recipe I know for coq au vin, the one in Julia Child's *The French Chef Cookbook*. Child's recipe, elaborate and correct, uses (and requires washing of) four cooking vessels. My streamlined version takes much less time, and lands you with just one pan to wash. Is hers better than mine? Of course. But having eaten both versions, I promise that mine will give great pleasure with far less trouble.

simplified coq au vin

serves 4

1–2 tablespoons vegetable
   oil
200g bacon or pancetta,
   thickly sliced and
   cut into thick shreds
   (lardons)
1 free-range chicken
   (about 1.5kg), cut into
   eight pieces
1 tablespoon cognac
2 tablespoons plain flour
1 tablespoon tomato purée
6 plump garlic cloves,
   thinly sliced
1 bay leaf
2 teaspoons herbes de
   Provence or similar
   herb mixture
4 onions (about 150g
   each)
500ml red wine (or white
   if that suits you better)
400ml chicken stock
300g button mushrooms,
   halved or quartered
large handful of fresh
   parsley, coarsely
   chopped
salt and freshly ground
   black pepper

Pour enough oil into the pressure cooker to film the base generously, then add the bacon or pancetta. Put it over a medium heat and cook, with regular stirring, until the bacon is lightly browned (about 3–4 minutes). Remove with a slotted spoon and put on a plate or heatproof dish that will also accommodate the chicken.

Put the chicken in the pan, four pieces at a time, and cook for just long enough to get a bit of colour into them; don't worry about deep or even browning. Cook the first batch, then the second, adding both to the plate or dish with the bacon.

Pour the cognac into the pan and let it sizzle down merrily, scraping the base of the pan, until it has reduced to nothingness. Season with salt and pepper, add the flour and a splash of water, and scrape the base of the pan thoroughly until the residues are amalgamated with the water and the whole mess has turned into a thick sludge. Add the tomato purée, garlic, bay leaf, herbs and onions, then put the chicken and bacon back into the pan. Pour in the liquids.

Clamp on the lid. Bring up to full pressure, turn the heat down to medium and cook for 10 minutes. Turn off the heat and vent the steam immediately. As soon as you can take the lid off, stir in the mushrooms. Turn the heat to low and cook until the mushrooms are just soft – about 5 minutes. Stir in the parsley, check the seasonings (you may need more salt and pepper), and serve with crusty bread, plain rice or new potatoes.

Couldn't be easier or faster. If you want to use breasts instead of leg, you will need just one piece per person. Start preparations the night before if possible.

jerk chicken

serves 4

8 chicken legs (thighs and/or drumsticks), skin off if you prefer
125ml jerk seasoning
3 tablespoons vegetable oil
juice of 1 lemon

Rub the chicken pieces all over with the seasoning, oil and lemon juice. Leave to marinate for a while – overnight in the fridge is ideal.

Heat up at least 7.5cm water in your pressure cooker with the steamer insert (or an improvised steamer rack) in place. Put the chicken pieces in the steamer. Clamp on the lid. Bring up to full pressure, turn the heat down to medium and cook for 10 minutes. Serve immediately with boiled rice and beans, if you like, and a salad.

chicken in a bowl

The pressure cooker excels with simple chicken dishes cooked by steaming in a bowl. Here are three examples. You will soon come up with your own once you've started using the method, and I promise your dinners à deux will never be the same. Remember, again: getting the water simmering before you begin preparation speeds up the arrival of your meal.

Sue me. I love cream. And I'll bet you do too, though you may be more likely to serve it with pudding (when guests come over) than use it in savoury dishes. But what happens when you serve your crumble or poached pears on Saturday night? There's a little bit of cream left over. This recipe lets you use up the leftovers. If there is no cream in the house, do not buy some just to make this dish. Use virtuous yoghurt instead, preferably Greek-style.

chicken with garlic-cream sauce

serves 2

2 plump garlic cloves, thinly sliced
1 bay leaf
4 chicken drumsticks, thighs or small breasts
4 tablespoons dry white wine
1 tablespoon double cream
salt and freshly ground black pepper
chopped fresh herbs, to garnish

Heat up at least 5cm water in your pressure cooker with the steamer insert (or an improvised steamer rack) in place. Put the garlic and bay leaf in a heatproof dish that will fit into your pressure cooker with at least 2.5cm of space between the dish and the side of the pan. Put in the chicken and pour over the wine and cream. Season with salt and freshly ground black pepper to taste. Put the bowl in the pressure cooker. Clamp on the lid. Bring up to full pressure, turn the heat down to medium and cook for 15 minutes. Garnish with the herbs and serve with rice or potatoes.

This is a satisfying midweek dinner when you want spice with minimal effort.

quickest chicken curry

serves 2

4 tablespoons Greek-style
yoghurt
2 teaspoons mild curry
powder
1 plump garlic clove,
finely chopped
1 shallot, thinly sliced
1 thin slice fresh root
ginger, finely chopped
4 chicken drumsticks,
thighs or small breasts
8–10 fresh coriander
sprigs, coarsely
chopped

Mix the yoghurt and curry powder in the heatproof dish
that you will be using to cook (one that will fit in your
pressure cooker with at least 2.5cm of space between
the dish and the side of the pan). Stir in the garlic, shallot
and ginger, and mix well, then add the chicken and coat
it thoroughly with the yoghurt mixture. Add 2 tablespoons
water to the dish.

Heat up at least 5cm water in your pressure cooker
with the steamer insert (or an improvised steamer rack)
in place. Put the dish in the steamer. Clamp on the lid.
Bring up to full pressure, turn the heat down to medium
and cook for 15 minutes. Turn off the heat and vent
immediately. Garnish with coriander and serve with rice
or potatoes.

This is food to eat with your fingers.

soy and chilli chicken

serves 2

2 chicken legs or breasts,
cut into 5cm chunks,
ideally through the bone
2 tablespoons soy sauce
1 tablespoon vegetable oil
2 plump garlic cloves,
finely chopped
2 thick slices fresh root
ginger, finely chopped
1 small chilli, de-seeded
if you wish, and finely
chopped
a large pinch of Chinese five-
spice powder (optional)
1 teaspoon sesame oil
2 spring onions, coarsely
chopped

Heat up at least 5cm water in your pressure cooker
with the steamer insert (or an improvised steamer rack)
in place. Put all the ingredients except the spring onion
into a heatproof dish that will fit in your steamer with at
least 2.5cm of space between the dish and the side of
the pan. Put the dish in the steamer. Clamp on the lid.
Bring up to full pressure, turn the heat down to medium
and cook for 15 minutes. Turn off the heat and vent
immediately. Garnish with the spring onions and serve
with rice.

Quail cook fast whichever method you use, and need careful treatment in the pressure cooker if they're not to dry out. I like this method because it gets some crunch into the skin by means of a quick spell in a hot pan when they come out of the pressure cooker.

quail with port and grapes

serves 4 (or 8 if
 preceded by a
 filling starter).

3 tablespoons vegetable
 oil
1 large onion (about
 250g), roughly chopped
2 tablespoons flour
8 quail
100ml ruby port
300ml chicken stock
1 teaspoon herbes de
 Provence or similar
 herb mixture
about 30 seedless red
 grapes
salt and freshly ground
 black pepper

Put 1 tablespoon vegetable oil and the onion in a frying pan and cook over a fairly brisk heat until very lightly coloured (about 5 minutes). Add the flour, plus a large splash of water, and stir in well. Season with salt and freshly ground black pepper and continue cooking until the flour has been absorbed by the onion, then cook for another 5 minutes or so, until the onion is soft. Remove to a bowl and wipe out the pan.

While the onions are cooking, put the quail, liquids and herbs in the pressure cooker. Season with salt and freshly ground black pepper. Clamp on the lid. Bring up to full pressure, turn the heat down to medium and cook for 10 minutes. Turn off the heat and vent immediately. Take the quail out as soon as you can. Add the grapes and onions to the pressure cooker and simmer gently for 5 minutes or so.

In the meantime, turn the heat on under the frying pan and add more vegetable oil. Brown the quail on both breasts quickly and lightly. To serve, put them on heated plates and pour some of the liquid over each plate, with the grapes scattered around. Serve immediately.

This simple recipe gives a great way to feed a crowd in little more than thirty minutes. The larger bird serves six, the smaller four.

pressure-poached chicken with salsa verde

serves 4–6

1 free-range chicken
(about 1.5–2kg)
1 bay leaf
1 garlic clove, unpeeled

For the salsa verde:
2 large handfuls of
fresh flat-leaf parsley,
leaves finely chopped
4–5 tablespoons capers,
finely chopped
1 can anchovy fillets,
well drained and
finely chopped
2–3 garlic cloves, finely
chopped
2 tablespoons red wine
vinegar
about 200ml extra
virgin olive oil

Put the chicken, bay leaf and garlic in the pressure cooker and pour in water to a depth of 5cm. Clamp on the lid. Bring up to full pressure, turn the heat down to medium and cook for 20 minutes for the smaller bird, 25 minutes for a larger one. Turn off the heat and vent immediately.

In the meantime, mix all the salsa ingredients together in a serving bowl.

Put the cooking liquid in a degreasing gravy boat and serve with the chicken. Serve with the salsa and with good bread or plain boiled rice.

Don't forget you can also use the cooking liquid for soup, or in the sauce for another chicken dish.

This is adapted from a recipe – which I've been cooking for more years than I care to remember – in *The Chinese Cookbook* by Craig Claiborne and Virginia Lee. The original contains no chilli; you can omit it if you wish. Cooked in an ordinary cooking vessel, wok or casserole, the dish needs at least thirty minutes. In the pressure cooker, it needs about ten. And by the way: save the wing tips to add to chicken stock.

chicken wings in tomato sauce

serves 4

2–3 tablespoons vegetable oil

20 chicken wings (about 1.5kg), tips removed and jointed

5–6 thick slices of fresh root ginger, finely chopped

4–5 garlic cloves, finely chopped

1–2 small chillies, de-seeded and finely chopped

2 × 400g cans chopped tomatoes

2 tablespoons Worcestershire sauce

4 tablespoons soy sauce

2 tablespoons red wine vinegar

2 teaspoons cornflour (optional)

small handful of fresh coriander, chopped

Pour oil into the pressure cooker to coat the base very generously. Put in half the wings and cook them over a medium-high heat, with regular stirring, to brown them lightly (about 3 minutes). Don't worry about even browning, which is both difficult and unnecessary. Remove to a plate and brown the second batch of wings, adding a little more oil if it's needed.

Put the wings back in the pan with all the remaining ingredients, except the cornflour. Stir to distribute the chopped items, then clamp on the lid. Bring up to full pressure, turn the heat down to medium and cook for 2 minutes. Turn off the heat and leave to vent gradually for 5 minutes before venting off the remaining steam. If the sauce is too thin, you can boil it down hard for a minute or two, or whisk 2 teaspoons of cornflour into an equal quantity of cooking liquid and then stir it into the contents of the pan. But a very wet sauce will merely add more tasty liquid for the white rice that makes the natural accompaniment. Stir in the coriander just before serving.

This is one of the all-time great chicken dishes, and perfectly suited to cooking in the pressure cooker.

chicken with 40 cloves of garlic

serves 6

125ml extra virgin olive oil
1 free-range chicken (about 2kg)
125ml dry white wine
125ml water or chicken stock
4 garlic bulbs, separated into cloves but unpeeled

Put enough of the oil in the pressure cooker to generously coat the base, and heat it to medium-hot. Turn the chicken in the oil for a few minutes, just long enough to colour it lightly. Put in all the remaining oil, the wine and the stock. Clamp on the lid. Bring up to full pressure, turn the heat down to medium, and cook for 15 minutes. Turn off the heat and vent immediately.

As soon as you can take the lid off, put the garlic in the pressure cooker. Clamp on the lid. Bring up to full pressure, turn the heat down to medium and cook for 5 minutes. Turn off the heat and vent immediately. Serve with crusty bread to soak up the heavenly juices, and some French beans or a green salad.

A hearty, traditional-style dish that's ready in under an hour and makes a complete meal. Save the cooking liquid for soup: it will be very tasty.

chicken with parsley dumplings

serves 4–6

1 free-range chicken
  (about 1.5–2kg)
1 bay leaf
1 garlic clove, unpeeled
4 celery sticks, sliced
  about 1.25cm thick
  diagonally
4 carrots, sliced
  about 1.25cm thick
  diagonally
2–3 small leeks, white
  parts only, sliced
  about 1.25cm thick
  diagonally
½ teaspoon dried mixed
  herbs

For the dumplings:
250g plain flour
1 teaspoon salt
2 teaspoons baking
  powder
2 tablespoons vegetable
  oil
small handful parsley,
  chopped
4–5 tablespoons fresh
  sage leaves, shredded
salt and freshly ground
  black pepper

Put the chicken, bay leaf and garlic in the pressure cooker and pour in water to a depth of 5cm. Clamp on the lid. Bring up to full pressure, turn the heat down to medium and cook for 20 minutes for a smaller bird, 25 minutes for a larger one. Turn off the heat and vent immediately.

As soon as you can lift the lid, remove the chicken carefully; take care to let as much liquid as possible drip back into the pressure cooker. Set the chicken aside and add the vegetables and dried herbs. Clamp on the lid. Bring up to full pressure, turn down the heat to medium and cook for 3 minutes. Turn off the heat and vent immediately.

Start preparing the dumplings in the meantime, as they are best made close to cooking time. Mix all the ingredients in a large bowl and season well with salt and freshly ground black pepper. Add just enough water (about 150ml) to make a stiff dough. Divide the dough into sixteen equal pieces and roll each gently to form a slightly flattened ball.

As soon as you can lift the lid, remove the vegetables with a slotted spoon. Turn the heat on under the pressure cooker to a gentle simmer. Drop the dumplings into the simmering pan and cook without pressure for about 15 minutes.

Meanwhile, cut up the chicken, if you like, and put it on a serving platter with the vegetables. Or just leave the chicken whole. Arrange the dumplings around the platter and serve immediately with a jug of the cooking liquid passed separately.

The garnish of avocado is a delicious surprise – as long as the avocado is of the Hass variety, and properly ripe. If you can't get that, just skip the avocado.

cuban-style chicken soup

serves 4

2–3 tablespoons
vegetable oil
500g free-range chicken
meat, cubed or thickly
sliced
1 litre chicken stock
(from cubes will be fine)
1 onion, quartered
1 teaspoon ground cumin
1 bay leaf
4 small waxy potatoes,
thickly sliced
50g orzo or another very
small pasta shape
8 cherry tomatoes,
halved
chopped fresh coriander,
to garnish (optional)
orange and avocado
slices, to serve

Pour some oil into the pressure cooker, using just enough to coat the base of the pan generously. Bring up to a brisk heat and put the chicken in, stir-frying just long enough to get a bit of colour into it (3–5 minutes). Pour in the stock and then all the remaining ingredients except the tomatoes. Clamp on the lid. Bring up to full pressure, turn the heat down to medium and cook for 5 minutes. Turn off the heat and vent immediately.

As soon as you can remove the lid, drop in the tomatoes and put the lid back on. Simmer without pressure just long enough to soften the tomatoes. Serve with the orange and avocado slices passed separately so that everyone can help themselves. You can also add chopped fresh coriander as a garnish, if you wish.

chicken stock

Making poultry stock (and meat stock, even more) takes a very long time. Hours are needed to extract all the flavour from those bones and their accompanying meat. And the cooking must be a gentle simmering or the stock will become cloudy. My friend John Whiting, who knows more about the pressure cooker than I ever will, doesn't mind cloudy stock – and that's why he makes it in the pressure cooker. I am a fetishist for perfectly clear stock, however, so I do the conventional simmering. The exception: boiling up a chicken or duck carcass when the bird has already been cooked. This is not 'proper' stock, in my view, and since I always use the stuff for everyday soups, cloudiness doesn't matter. Method: chop the carcass into four or five pieces, using all the scraps, and chuck it in the pressure cooker with a carrot, a celery stalk, some garlic, some dried herbs, and a halved onion. Put in water to cover, then clamp on the lid. Bring up to full pressure, turn the heat down to medium and cook for 5 minutes. Turn off the heat and leave to vent gradually. Strain off the solids and you're done.

Based on a recipe in Sri Owen's *Noodles: The New Way*.

indonesian chicken soup with egg noodles

serves 4

4 chicken quarters, leg (best bet) or breast
1 litre light chicken stock or water
250g packet of egg noodles
100g beansprouts
a few fresh parsley sprigs, finely chopped
1 spring onion, finely chopped
4 slices of lemon, to garnish

For the spice paste:
1 large onion, finely chopped
3 plump garlic cloves, finely chopped
2.5cm piece of fresh root ginger, finely chopped
5 blanched almonds, finely chopped
¼ teaspoon turmeric
1 teaspoon chilli powder
2 tablespoons vegetable oil

To make the spice paste, put all the paste ingredients in a blender with a splash of water. Blend until smooth and scrape into a bowl. Set aside.

Put the chicken pieces in the pressure cooker with the chicken stock or water. Clamp on the lid. Bring up to full pressure, turn the heat down to medium and cook for 5 minutes. Turn off the heat and vent immediately. When the chicken is cool enough to handle, take it off the bone and cut or tear into small pieces; keep the bones. Strain the cooking liquid into a pan or jug and set aside.

Put the spice paste in the pressure cooker and heat gently, with constant stirring, for a couple of minutes. Put the chicken meat and bones back into the pressure cooker and pour in the reserved stock. Clamp on the lid. Bring up to full pressure, turn the heat down to medium and cook for 3 minutes. Turn off the heat and vent immediately.

In the meantime, cook the noodles according to the instructions on the packet but make sure they stay slightly short of fully cooked. Drain well, rinse under the cold tap, and set aside.

As soon as you can lift the lid from the pressure cooker, remove the bones, then put in the noodles and bean sprouts and let them heat for a minute. Spoon the soup into four bowls, top each with the parsley, spring onions and a lemon slice, and serve immediately.

This is something like a meatloaf, and it's good. You must use the best chicken thighs you can get your hands on, and do try to mince them yourself.

herby chicken loaf

serves 3–4

800g free-range minced
  chicken or 1kg free-
  range chicken thighs
a large handful of dried
  breadcrumbs
a small handful each of
  fresh parsley and mint,
  finely chopped
2 plump garlic cloves,
  finely chopped
2 thick slices of onion,
  roughly chopped
1 tablespoon vegetable oil
2 tablespoons dry white
  wine
salt and freshly ground
  black pepper

Heat up at least 5cm water in your pressure cooker with the steamer insert (or an improvised steamer rack) in place.

If you are mincing the chicken yourself, remove the skin and cut out the bones, then chop them coarsely using two big knives or (if you must) a food processor.

Put the chicken in a heatproof dish that will fit into your steamer with at least 2.5cm of space between the dish and the side of the pan. Season with salt and freshly ground black pepper, and mix well with all the remaining ingredients (easiest with your hands).

Put the dish in the steamer. Clamp on the lid. Bring up to full pressure, turn the heat down to medium and cook for 20 minutes. Turn off the heat and vent immediately. Serve hot with good bread or mashed potatoes.

My mother, a wonderful cook, used to make a delicious duck dish for dinner parties. After her death, while going through her books, I found her recipe in *Ess Gezunterhayt*, a charity booklet published in the early 1960s. *Ess Gezunterhayt* (or *Gezunterhait*) in Yiddish means 'eat in good health'. Note: this is an old-fashioned, falling-off-the-bone rendition of duck.

my mother's duck casserole

serves 4

1 medium duck
  (1.75–2.25kg)
2–3 tablespoons
  vegetable oil for
  browning
12 small white onions
  or shallots, peeled but
  left whole
2 tablespoons flour
3 tablespoons cognac or
  another good brandy
100ml dry white wine
250ml chicken or duck
  stock
1 bouquet garni or 1
  teaspoon dried mixed
  herbs, such as herbes
  de Provence
1 teaspoon tomato purée
1 carrot
12 small button
  mushrooms
salt and freshly ground
  black pepper
small handful of fresh
  parsley, finely chopped,
  to garnish

Joint the duck or have the butcher joint it for you. The legs should be jointed into thigh and drumstick. The breast should be cut in two. The wings should have their tips taken off. Use the trimmings to make duck stock or, if you prefer, put them in the pressure cooker along with the pieces you'll be serving.

Pour enough oil into the pressure cooker just to coat the base of the pan generously. Season the duck with salt and freshly ground black pepper, and turn the heat to medium-high. Brown a few pieces lightly, as evenly as you can, then remove to a plate and brown the remainder. Now brown the onions and remove to a plate. Pour out the excess oil, leaving about 2 tablespoons in the pressure cooker.

Return the pressure cooker to the heat and stir in the flour. When it is thoroughly mixed into the fat, add the cognac and then the wine, stock, herbs and tomato purée. Bring to the boil and put in the duck pieces and the carrot. Clamp on the lid. Bring up to full pressure, turn the heat down to medium and cook for 20 minutes. Turn off the heat and vent immediately.

While the duck is cooking, put the onions or shallots into a pan with water or stock to cover. Simmer at a fairly brisk pace for 15 minutes, then drain them. Put the onions and the mushrooms in the pressure cooker. Clamp on the lid. Bring up to full pressure, turn the heat down to medium and cook for 5 minutes more. Remove all the solid ingredients from the pressure cooker, setting the carrot aside.

Put the carrot in a fine sieve and mash it back into the pressure cooker. Stir into the cooking liquid to blend well. Taste the liquid. If it is too dilute, boil it down briskly. If there isn't enough of it, add some stock or water. Serve with rice or mashed potatoes and sprinkle with parsley.

The term 'confit' is misused frequently in recipes and menus. True confit de canard is a duck leg cooked slowly in duck fat for long storage submerged in the fat, and it isn't something you can easily do unless you have access to massive quantities of the fat. But this speedy steamed approximation is very good and, like confit, it can be fried briefly after cooking to crisp up the skin. Allow one leg per person.

'confit' duck

serves 4

4 duck legs, excess fat removed but reserved
½ teaspoon herbes de Provence or similar herb mixture
1 bay leaf
1 plump garlic clove, peeled but left whole
2 tablespoons dry white wine
salt and freshly ground black pepper

Rub the duck on the flesh side with the herbs, a little salt, and a good grinding of pepper. Chill for an hour or two if you can – this enables the flesh to absorb some flavour from the herbs, salt and pepper.

Heat up at least 5cm water in your pressure cooker with the steamer insert (or an improvised steamer rack) in place. Put the duck in a heatproof dish that will fit in your pressure cooker with at least 2.5cm of space between the dish and the side of the pan. Tuck the bay leaf and garlic under the pieces and pour in the wine. Clamp on the lid. Bring up to full pressure, turn the heat down to medium and cook for 10 minutes. Turn off the heat and vent immediately, then leave the duck to cool, and chill if not using immediately.

Use the reserved fat for frying or roasting potatoes, or for adding flavour to pressure-cooked vegetables.

part-cooked duck for two

You can make a very good duck dish by part-cooking the breast or legs and then finishing them in a frying pan. Pressure cook for 5 minutes only, vent immediately, and cook over a moderate heat in a non-stick frying pan for 2–3 minutes per side, just long enough to brown them. While you're browning the duck, you can utilise the heat in the pressure cooker by cooking some simple vegetables such as French beans or courgettes.

This is Chinese in inspiration, both the flavours and the method of chopping the duck. The ideal approach: get it started the day before you plan to eat, so those spicy flavours will have a chance to mellow. A joyful mess to eat, if you do it right. If you don't have a meat cleaver, I will forgive you for asking the butcher to cut up the bird.

five-spice duck

serves 4

1 small duck (about 1.75kg)
2 teaspoons Chinese five-spice powder
1 teaspoon freshly ground black pepper
¼ teaspoon mild chilli powder
2 teaspoons Chinese rice wine or dry sherry
2 teaspoons soy sauce

Cut the duck up, or ask your butcher to do it for you (wimp!), as follows. Joint into four pieces. Cut off the backbone and chop through the bone into pieces about 5cm square. Chop the breasts crosswise into pieces of comparable size. Joint the legs and chop both drumsticks and thighs into two pieces.

Heat up at least 5cm water in your pressure cooker with the steamer insert (or an improvised steamer rack) in place. Put the duck in a heatproof dish that will fit in your steamer with at least 2.5cm of space between the dish and the side of the pan. Add all the remaining ingredients and toss thoroughly (easiest with your bare hands). Put the dish in the steamer. Clamp on the lid. Bring up to full pressure, turn the heat down to medium and cook for 10 minutes. Turn off the heat and vent immediately.

You can now complete the cooking immediately or wait a day. If you're waiting, leave the duck to cool and then cover and chill.

To complete cooking: preheat your grill until it's blazing hot. In the meantime, put the duck pieces flesh side up in the grill pan. Grill for just long enough to get the meat sizzling (about 3–5 minutes), then turn and cook until the skin is brown and crisp. Serve immediately with rice or noodles, and insist that your guests eat the duck with their fingers.

The bird can be browned in the pressure cooker but use a frying pan if you prefer.

guinea fowl with orange and spices

serves 2–3

1 guinea fowl
2–3 tablespoons vegetable oil
1 large onion, thickly sliced
2 whole cloves
1 piece of cinnamon stick
2 allspice berries
2 juniper berries
2 large pieces of orange peel, fresh or dried
2 tablespoons plain flour
400ml stock or water
50ml dry white wine
salt and freshly ground black pepper
watercress, to garnish (optional)

Brown the bird lightly in just enough oil to cover the base of a heavy pan (or the pressure cooker if you wish). You can't brown every single bit of it, but doing both breasts and the back will suffice. Transfer to the pressure cooker if you've used a frying pan for browning. Put the onion in the pressure cooker around the bird, followed by the spices, orange peel and flour, distributing both well over the onions. Add 350ml of the stock or water and season with salt and pepper.

Clamp on the lid. Bring up to full pressure, turn the heat down to medium and cook for 20 minutes if you like poultry à point (just done), 25 minutes if you like it closer to the falling-off-the-bone stage. Turn off the heat and vent immediately.

While the bird is resting, pour the remaining stock and the wine into the pressure cooker and simmer vigorously for 10 minutes or so. Serve with rice or potatoes and with a garnish of watercress, if you like.

This is a dish for summer or early autumn, when the tomatoes are red, ripe and deeply flavourful. You could make it with canned tomatoes at other times of the year, and the dish will taste good. But not quite as good. Note: if you can't get a guinea fowl, a small chicken would also work well.

pan roast guinea fowl with tomatoes and herbs

serves 3–4

2–3 tablespoons vegetable oil
1 guinea fowl or small free-range chicken (about 1–1.5kg)
1 large onion, roughly chopped
1 tablespoon flour
6 plump garlic cloves, roughly chopped
125ml dry white wine
125ml water or chicken stock
4 red, ripe tomatoes, quartered
2–3 fresh thyme sprigs
2–3 small fresh rosemary sprigs
4–5 bay leaves, preferably in a single sprig
8–10 ripe cherry tomatoes, halved
salt and freshly ground black pepper
8–10 basil leaves, torn into small pieces, to garnish

Put enough of the oil in the pressure cooker to generously coat the base, and heat it to medium-hot. Turn the bird in the oil for a few minutes, just long enough to colour it lightly. Remove to a plate.

Add a little more oil if needed and cook the onion and flour, stirring regularly, just long enough to colour it lightly (4–5 minutes). Now put the bird back in the pan followed by all the remaining ingredients, except the cherry tomatoes. Season with salt and freshly ground black pepper. Clamp the lid on, bring up to full pressure, turn the heat down to medium and cook for 20 minutes. Turn off the heat and vent immediately.

As soon as you can take the lid off, remove the bird to a deep serving platter. Turn the heat back on to a gentle simmer and add the cherry tomatoes. Cook for just long enough to soften them slightly (about 4–5 minutes). Spoon the contents of the pressure cooker around the bird and sprinkle on the basil. Serve with crusty bread or plain boiled rice.

starch

The pressure cooker produces several starchy dishes – potatoes for mashing, pulses, plain rice, risotto – that are indistinguishable from their counterparts cooked conventionally. Indistinguishable in every sense, that is, except one: they take a small fraction of the time to cook. I'm especially keen on cooking pulses this way, as they can take as little as five minutes. Throw in some spices and a small piece of lamb or chicken, and you can eat a full meal within 15 minutes of arriving home. Rice cooked under pressure is just as good, and using the method here has the added advantage of giving you a lovely way of serving the rice with no extra effort. Best of all, in many people's view, will be the risotto. Remember the old line about having to stir, stir, stir for the better part of an hour? Hogwash. Do it in the pressure cooker, which takes very little time and eliminates most of the stirring.

I used to think that pressure cooker rice was a waste of time, since cooking rice in the conventional way is so easy and fast. *Miss Vickie's Big Book of Pressure Cooker Recipes*, by Vickie Smith, changed my mind. I tried her method and it worked perfectly. The time from uncooked to readiness is not significantly shorter than the conventional method but it is a little shorter. And it gives you an attractive presentation with no trouble.

rice

serves 6

400ml long grain rice

Wash the rice in three or four changes of cold water, until the water runs fairly clear after draining; this removes some of the surface starch and guarantees good separation of the grains.

Put the rice in a fairly deep bowl with a capacity of 1 or 1.5 litres – one that will accommodate the rice when it doubles or trebles in volume, but which will fit into your steamer while leaving a gap of 2.5cm between the bowl and the side of the pan. Pour in 600ml of water, or light chicken stock if you have some.

Heat up at least 5cm water in your pressure cooker with the steamer insert (or an improvised steamer rack) in place. Put the bowl in the steamer. Clamp on the lid. Bring up to full pressure, turn the heat down to medium and cook for 4 minutes. Turn the heat off and leave to vent gradually. Serve from the bowl, or turn the rice out onto a serving platter in an attractive mound, which you can then surround with vegetables, a curry, or whatever you're cooking.

more interesting rice

To get more flavour into the rice, mix in small but tasty extras before cooking.
Such as:

1–2 plump garlic cloves, finely chopped
1–2 thin slices fresh root ginger, peeled and finely chopped
½ teaspoon herbes de Provence or similar herb mixture
1 teaspoon whole spices, such as coriander, cumin or fennel seed
1 teaspoon tomato purée

This recipe was first published in my book *The Green Kitchen*. It is reproduced exactly here, for the simple reason that I can't find any way of improving on it.

basic risotto

serves 3–4 as a side dish

1 small onion, finely chopped
a good knob of butter, or a smaller knob with 1 tablespoon or so of extra virgin olive oil
250g Arborio rice
600ml homemade chicken stock
small handful of fresh parsley, finely chopped
freshly grated Parmesan, to taste
salt and freshly ground black pepper

Put the onion and butter or butter and oil in the pressure cooker over a gentle heat. Sweat the onion (i.e., cook it without colouring it) for a few minutes, just to soften it slightly and take away the raw flavour. Now add the rice and stir into the onions to coat it well and get a sheen of translucence in the grains. This will take 2–3 minutes.

Add the stock, a little salt and a lot of pepper. Clamp on the lid. Bring up to full pressure, turn the heat down to medium and cook for 5 minutes. Turn off the heat and vent immediately, then remove the lid as soon as possible. Stir in the chopped parsley and a little cheese, and leave, with the lid slightly ajar, to finish cooking for 2–3 minutes. Everyone can add extra cheese as they see fit.

risotto variations

The basic risotto is so easy in the pressure cooker, and you can perform numerous variations that make it even more splendid.

Peas and rice make a great partnership, and frozen peas – as always – are just as good as fresh (if not better). Use parsley if you don't have basil.

risotto with peas and basil

serves 2–3 as a main
   course, 4–6 as a
   starter

1 quantity basic risotto
250g frozen peas
8–10 basil leaves,
   roughly torn

Make the risotto and cook the peas while it is cooking (easiest in the microwave). Add to the pressure cooker when the risotto is cooked and leave in the pan so that they can heat through. Sprinkle on the basil before serving.

I love lightly cooked scallops, and this recipe gets them that way without using direct heat.

risotto with chilli, scallops and lime

serves 2–3 as a main
   course, 4–6 as a
   starter

1 quantity basic risotto
250g scallops, sliced
   6mm thick
1 small piece of fresh
   red chilli, about
   1.25cm in length,
   de-seeded if you wish,
   finely chopped
juice of ½ lime

Mix the scallops, chilli and lime juice, and leave in the fridge for an hour or two. Add to the pressure cooker when the risotto is cooked and leave in the pot so they can heat through. Note: the scallops will be barely cooked. If you want them more done, cook quickly in a small pan or the microwave for a minute or so before adding to the risotto.

The prawns can be frozen, which makes this an elegant but practical dinner party dish.

risotto with lemon prawns

serves 2–3 as a main course, 4–6 as a starter

250g cooked, shelled prawns (defrosted if frozen)
juice and grated zest of ½ a lemon
1 small garlic clove, finely chopped
1 quantity of basic risotto (page 98)
fresh chopped parsley, to garnish

Mix the prawns, lemon juice and zest, and the garlic, and leave in the fridge for an hour or two. Make the risotto as described on page 98. Add the prawn mixture to the pressure cooker when the risotto is cooked and leave in the pan so that they can heat through. Garnish with parsley.

I used to think that the fastest and easiest way to cook polenta was in the microwave. I was wrong. The pressure cooker beats it. You're restricted in the quantity you can cook under pressure because care is needed with starchy things not to overfill: the grains can clog the valve and cause problems. But the quantity here will feed six as a side dish, so you won't suffer too much.

polenta

serves 6

175g polenta (coarse
   cornmeal)
1 litre water
1 teaspoon salt
2 tablespoons extra
   virgin olive oil

Put all the ingredients, except the oil, in the pressure cooker and turn the heat to high. Stir with a whisk constantly until the mixture starts to bubble energetically (3–5 minutes). Clamp on the lid. Bring up to full pressure, turn the heat down to medium and cook for 5 minutes. Turn off the heat and vent immediately.

As soon as you can take the lid off, pour in the oil and whisk thoroughly. Serve as it is, or spread the polenta out in a flat-based dish and leave to cool for slicing and grilling, frying or baking.

variation

Use 50g butter instead of the olive oil and you will have the southern American dish called grits. Grits are always eaten soft, sometimes with grated cheese mixed in (cheese grits, a tasty dish). Use a sharp Cheddar if you're doing the cheesy thing.

The pressure cooker greatly speeds up the cooking of mashed potatoes. It also leaves the potatoes drier than conventional methods. Here is the basic method, with a couple of ways of using your potatoes once they're mashed. Note: you can cook large quantities in this way as long as you don't fill the pressure cooker more than two thirds of the way up.

mashed potato

serves 4–6

1kg floury potatoes, such as King Edwards or Maris Piper, peeled and cut into chunks about 2.5cm square
100–200g butter
300–400ml milk
salt and freshly ground black pepper

Put the potatoes on the steamer insert (or an improvised steamer rack) with about 7.5cm water in the base of the pressure cooker. Clamp on the lid. Bring up to full pressure, turn the heat down to medium and cook for 10 minutes. Turn off the heat and vent immediately. When the lid can be lifted, remove the potatoes and pour out the water. Put the potatoes back in the pressure cooker over a low heat. Add butter to taste, mixing in thoroughly, and season with salt and freshly ground black pepper. Now add enough milk to get the consistency you like. The mash can be left with the heat off and covered for a couple of hours if that suits your schedule.

This famous Irish dish is a true delicacy when made with good potatoes, good cabbage and good butter. Even if the ingredients are just ordinary, the dish is still good.

colcannon

serves 6

500g floury potatoes, such as King Edwards or Maris Piper, peeled and cut into chunks about 2.5cm square
1 small white or green cabbage, thickly sliced
150–200ml milk
50–100g butter
salt and freshly ground black pepper

Cook the potatoes as above. When the lid can be lifted, remove the potatoes to another pan but retain the water.

Put the cabbage in the pressure cooker. Clamp on the lid. Bring up to full pressure, turn the heat down to medium and cook for 3 minutes. Turn off the heat and vent immediately. In the meantime, mash the potatoes with about half the milk and butter.

Drain the cabbage of excess water and add to the potatoes. Season with salt and freshly ground black pepper and add enough milk and butter to make a creamy consistency; don't worry about getting all the lumps out. If you want to be authentic and traditional, you can add more butter in a well in the top of the potatoes before serving. Serve immediately.

This other famous Irish dish is perfectly simple but really distinguished. I think you could easily double the quantity of spring onions. They make the dish what it is.

champ

serves 6

1 quantity Mashed
   Potato (page 103),
   without butter or milk
10–12 spring onions,
   roughly chopped
400ml milk
about 100g butter, to
   taste
salt and freshly ground
   black pepper

While the potatoes are cooking, put the spring onions and milk in a small pan. Bring to the boil, turn off the heat and leave until the potatoes are ready.

When the potatoes are ready, drain and mash but do not add milk or butter. Mix in the spring onions and their milk, then season and add butter to taste – start with about 100g of butter and add more as needed. If you want to be authentic and traditional, you can add more butter into a well in the top of the potatoes before serving.

A wonderful side dish or a main course for vegetarians.

dhal

serves 4 as a main
  course, 6 as a side
  dish

300g yellow split peas
1 small onion, finely
  chopped
2 tablespoons vegetable
  oil
5 plump garlic cloves,
  finely chopped
1 or 2 small chillies,
  de-seeded and finely
  chopped
3 thick slices fresh root
  ginger, finely chopped
½ teaspoon ground
  turmeric
finely chopped coriander
  and/or crisply fried
  onions, to garnish

Soak the peas in water while you prepare the other ingredients. Put the onion in the pressure cooker with the vegetable oil and fry briskly for a few minutes, just to get it smelling really great and getting a bit of colour into it. Add the garlic, chillies and ginger, and cook for a few minutes more, taking care not to let the garlic get too brown (it could taste bitter if you do).

Drain the peas and add them to the pressure cooker with the turmeric. Stir well, then pour in 750ml water. Clamp on the lid. Bring up to full pressure and turn the heat down to medium.

You can cook these pulses in one of two ways. If you want them very soft, cook for 10 minutes. If you want them to hold together better, cook for 5 minutes. And you can split the difference by starting out with 5 minutes and then venting and tasting. If the peas are still a little crunchy, cook for a few minutes more under pressure. Turn off the heat and vent immediately.

The dhal can now be mashed up to give it a creamy consistency, but I don't think that's necessary. If the mixture seems too dry – dhal should be almost soupy – add water to taste. Garnish, if you wish, with finely chopped coriander and/or some onions fried to crispness in vegetable oil.

pulses

Once you've cooked pulses in a pressure cooker, you'll see that there's little reason to use any other method. Cooking times in an open pan range from 45 minutes to 2 hours (or even more if the pulses are very old). The pressure cooker cuts this to 10 minutes or less. The only snag: over-filling the pressure cooker is especially dangerous when there are pulses inside, because the starchy liquid is just the sort of stuff that can clog the vent. Avoid at all costs. The two-thirds rule is never more important than with pulses. Pulses for cooking in the pressure cooker need to be soaked before cooking, except for split red lentils. Either soak them overnight in cold water or pour boiling water over the beans and leave for an hour or two. Drain and rinse.

timing pulses

Different sources give different timings for the various types of pulse. It's all very confusing, and I don't think the confusion is necessary. In my experience, using all kinds of pulses, I've found that they all cook in about the same time.

There is just one slight trick to pressure-cooked pulses. It is best to vent gradually and leave the pressure to return to normal by slow release. The extra time completes cooking without extra energy use. But if you're in a hurry, you can dispense with the slow release by adding a couple of minutes to the cooking times here.

As always with the pressure cooker, if the pulses are not done when you pop the lid off, just put it back on and give them a few minutes more. This may be necessary if the pulses are very old at the time of purchase, and there is no way to tell until you've cooked them.

cooking times:

- Larger whole pulses (such as cannellini beans or chickpeas)
  8–10 minutes for softness
  6–7 minutes for al dente

- Hulled pulses (such as red or yellow lentils)
  4–5 minutes

- Small whole pulses (such as lentilles de Puy)
  5–6 minutes

Your preference will depend on what the pulses are for. If they will be cooked again, or if they're for a salad, al dente is good. If you want them soft and mushy, so you get some of the internal starch coming out to thicken the liquid, then the longer time is probably right.

If you're making beans in the pressure cooker, you can just cook them in water or stock until soft. For a very little extra effort, however, you can add flavour to them at the first stage. Here is my basic procedure. Use duck fat, bacon fat, vegetable oil or olive oil. And while the stock should be homemade if possible, don't fret if you have to use cubes.

basic braised beans

serves 4–6

500g white or cannellini
  beans, soaked
  overnight
2 carrots, finely chopped
1 small leek, white only,
  finely chopped
3 celery sticks, finely
  chopped
2 garlic cloves, finely
  chopped
2 tablespoons oil or fat
1 teaspoon herbes de
  Provence or similar
  herb mixture
1 large bay leaf
about 1 litre unsalted
  stock

Drain the beans. Put all the ingredients, except the beans and stock, in the pressure cooker, and sweat them (i.e., cook gently without colouring) for 3–4 minutes, stirring a few times. When they're smelling very fragrant, mix in the beans. Pour in the stock, making sure there is enough to cover the beans by about 2.5cm. Add water if necessary, but remember: don't fill the pan by more than two thirds or three quarters, depending on the manufacturer's instructions. Clamp on the lid. Bring up to full pressure, turn the heat down to medium and cook for 8 minutes if you're eating beans immediately, 6 minutes if they will be cooked in another dish. Turn off the heat and leave to vent gradually.

beans and a bone

Every cuisine where meat is eaten has at least one recipe combining a hunk of meat (usually on a bone) with a potful of beans. This kind of dish gives the flavour of the meat without giving too much of the meat itself – a good way of eating meat – and involves far less expense than a roast or most braises. And, needless to say, this kind of dish is perfect for the pressure cooker. To make it, use the preceding recipe but first pressure cook your meat. My list of candidates would include:

pig's trotters (one per person)
lamb shanks (ditto)
a smoked pork knuckle, or 2 if they are small
a knuckle of uncooked ham, soaked if it is very salty

To adapt them for my basic braised beans, cook the meat in the pressure cooker first for 20 minutes with 500ml water. Turn off the heat and vent immediately. Test it: it should be just short of fully cooked. Remove the meat and the liquid, saving the liquid for cooking the dish (unless it is very salty) or for a soup. Now proceed with the braised beans, but put the meat on top for cooking under pressure.

vegetables

Like many people, I long advocated steaming as the method of choice for simple cooking of vegetables; now I am far more likely to use the pressure cooker. Pressure cookers do the job faster. Although you have to watch the timing carefully if you don't want them to overcook, the gain in speed is considerable. And the pressure cooker can accommodate a larger quantity than all but the most capacious steamers, so it's ideal when you're cooking for a crowd. For steaming you need a pressure cooker with a steamer insert, which is included with most new pressure cookers nowadays. If yours doesn't have one, improvise with the steamer insert from another pan, upended if necessary, or with a free-standing insert or small colander. And you don't have to use the pressure cooker for simple vegetable dishes only. This chapter has a few ideas for more elaborate dishes.

general notes on vegetables

In nearly all cases, the procedure for simple cooking of vegetables is the same. Put the vegetables in the steamer insert of the pressure cooker with 5–7.5cm of water in the base. Clamp on the lid. Bring up to full pressure, turn the heat down to medium and cook for the specified period. Turn off the heat and vent immediately. As soon as you can take off the lid, test to see if the vegetables are done. If not, clamp the lid back on and cook without pressure for a few more minutes.

Here are the cooking times that I've established for my own pressure cooker. Yours may differ slightly, and you will have to figure it out through trial and error – though your pressure cooker is likely to include some recipes that will guide you. In all cases, except where noted, the timings are for al dente vegetables.

A final note: the water used for steaming is useful stuff. It will have a pronounced taste of whatever you cooked over it, and can be added to soups and stews.

cooking times

Vegetable	Cooking time	Release
Cabbage	2 minutes	Immediate
Carrots	3 minutes	Immediate
Celery	2 minutes	Immediate
Fennel	2 minutes	Immediate
French beans	2 minutes	Immediate
Leeks	2 minutes	Immediate
Parsnips	5 minutes	Immediate
Corn on the cob	5 minutes	Immediate
Globe artichokes	15–25 minutes	Immediate
Small cubes or thick slices of squash or pumpkin, or whole small squash	4–5 minutes	Immediate

Really simple and really good.

buttered carrots with ginger

serves 4

450g smallish carrots,
topped and tailed,
peeled if you wish,
and left whole
50g butter
2 thick slices fresh
root ginger, finely
chopped
200ml chicken stock
(or water)
1–2 teaspoons lemon
juice or red wine
vinegar
salt and freshly ground
black pepper
chopped fresh
coriander, to garnish

Put all the ingredients, except the lemon juice or vinegar, in the pressure cooker and season with salt and freshly ground black pepper. Clamp on the lid. Bring up to full pressure, turn the heat down to medium and cook for 3–5 minutes. The shorter time will leave them with a good hint of al dente bite, the longer time softens them completely. Sprinkle on the lemon juice or vinegar just before serving, and garnish, if you wish, with chopped coriander.

This is a dish from the state of Mississippi, which I have adapted from Sheila Hibben's *Regional American Cookery* (1932). Hibben suggests serving it with fried chicken, and that sounds like a great idea to me. Use vegetable oil instead of the bacon fat if you insist, but the dish won't be quite as good.

sweetcorn, okra and tomatoes

serves 4–6 as a side dish

6 spring onions, finely chopped

3 green peppers, de-seeded and roughly chopped

2 tablespoons bacon fat or vegetable oil

500g okra, left whole

2 x 400g cans chopped tomatoes

250g frozen sweetcorn

1 teaspoon sugar

salt and freshly ground black pepper

Put the spring onions and peppers in the pressure cooker with the fat or oil. Cook over a low heat, stirring regularly, until the onions are fragrant and slightly soft (about 5 minutes). Add the okra and toss it well in the oil, then season with salt and freshly ground black pepper. Now add the tomatoes. Clamp on the lid. Bring up to full pressure, turn the heat down to medium and cook for 10 minutes. Turn off the heat and vent immediately. Test a piece of okra; if it's still a little chewy, cook for another couple of minutes. Otherwise just add the sweetcorn and put the lid back on. Heat for another minute or so, without pressure, until the sweetcorn is just done. Serve immediately.

My favourite treatment for green, white or Savoy cabbage takes forty-five minutes to oven-cook but only fifteen in the pressure cooker.

braised spiced cabbage

serves 4–6

3 tablespoons vegetable oil

½ teaspoon each whole cumin, coriander and fennel seeds

3 garlic cloves, finely chopped

1 large cabbage (about 1kg), cored and thickly sliced

300ml chicken or meat stock

salt and freshly ground black pepper

Put the oil in the pressure cooker. Heat the spices and garlic gently until they start smelling good (about 3–5 minutes), then put in all the remaining ingredients. Season and toss thoroughly. Clamp on the lid, bring to full pressure, turn the heat down to medium and cook for 5 minutes. Turn off the heat and vent immediately if you want the cabbage to retain a bit of bite. If you want it soft, leave it to vent gradually. Serve piping hot or at room temperature.

This is really more of a stew than a traditional sautéed ratatouille, but it tastes just as good and takes around one tenth the cooking time.

simple ratatouille

serves 4–6

600g aubergines, cut into 2.5cm cubes

600g courgettes, cut into 2.5cm chunks

3 plump garlic cloves, roughly chopped

1 large onion, roughly chopped

400g can chopped tomatoes

1 tablespoon vegetable oil

1 teaspoon herbes de Provence or similar herb mixture

small handful of basil, coarsely chopped

2 tablespoons extra virgin olive oil

Put all the ingredients, except the olive oil and basil, in the pressure cooker. Clamp on the lid. Bring up to full pressure, turn the heat down to medium and cook for 5 minutes. Turn off the heat and vent immediately. Check the vegetables; if the aubergines are still a little chewy, put the lid back on and cook for a minute more. When you're ready to serve, stir in the extra virgin olive oil and the basil. Good hot or at room temperature.

This is amazingly simple and amazingly good. The only trick lies in buying small aubergines, as the big ones don't cook quickly enough when cooked whole. Leaving them whole preserves all the flavour and the juiciness.

steamed aubergines with sesame dressing

serves 4

8 or 12 baby aubergines, about 10cm long
1½ tablespoons vegetable oil
1 teaspoon sesame oil
2 teaspoons soy sauce
2 teaspoons red wine or cider vinegar
1 thin slice fresh root ginger, finely chopped
2 spring onions, finely chopped
a small handful of fresh coriander, finely chopped
1 teaspoon sesame seeds
freshly ground black pepper

Heat up 7.5cm water in your pressure cooker with the steamer insert (or an improvised steamer rack) in place. Put the aubergines in the steamer. Clamp on the lid. Bring up to full pressure, turn the heat down to medium and cook for 5 minutes. Leave to vent gradually.

In the meantime, make the dressing by mixing all the ingredients except the coriander and sesame seeds. Season with freshly ground black pepper – no salt for now, because soy sauce is salty.

When you are ready to serve, split the aubergines lengthwise, leaving the stem on each one. Spread out on a serving platter and distribute the dressing and coriander evenly over them. Heat the sesame seeds in a small dry frying pan until they're just starting to colour. Sprinkle onto the aubergines and serve immediately.

simple steamed aubergines

If you love aubergines as much as I do, you will be happy to eat them sometimes all on their own, with nothing more than a sprinkling of coarse salt and black pepper. Here is the way to do it with medium-sized aubergines weighing about 200g.

Heat up 7.5cm water in your pressure cooker with the steamer insert (or an improvised steamer rack) in place. Put the whole aubergines in the steamer. Clamp on the lid. Bring up to full pressure, turn the heat down to medium and cook for 5 minutes. Turn off the heat and vent immediately.

If the aubergines you buy are larger, they can be cut in half lengthwise and cooked in the same way

Whole courgettes in the pressure cooker steam beautifully, retaining all their inner juice and avoiding the sogginess that can creep in when they're sliced before cooking. And they do it in less than half the time needed for conventional steaming. Here is a simple, summery salad. If you prefer, you can eat them plain, or slice them thickly and sauté quickly with garlic and extra virgin olive oil. This is a great party dish.

courgette salad with cherry tomatoes

serves 6–8

1 tablespoon red wine vinegar
1 small garlic clove, peeled and smashed
10 courgettes (about 750g total weight), left whole
2 tablespoons extra virgin olive oil
1 tablespoon vegetable oil
12–16 cherry tomatoes, halved
1 small red onion, thinly sliced
8–10 fresh basil sprigs, roughly torn
salt and freshly ground black pepper
coarse salt, to garnish (optional)

At least one hour before you plan to eat, put the vinegar and garlic in a bowl with a good seasoning of salt. The vinegar will pick up the garlic flavour – but not too much of it.

Heat up 7.5cm water in your pressure cooker with the steamer insert (or an improvised steamer rack) in place. Put the courgettes in the steamer. Clamp on the lid. Bring up to full pressure, turn the heat down to medium and cook for 5 minutes. Turn off the heat and vent immediately. Take out the courgettes, and leave them to cool for 5–10 minutes. Remove the garlic from the vinegar, whisk in the oils, and season with salt and freshly ground black pepper.

When the courgettes are just warm to the touch, top and tail them. Slice fairly thickly (about 1.25cm) diagonally and place on a serving platter. Put the tomatoes and then the onion slices on top. Sprinkle on the vinaigrette evenly, scatter the basil on top, and serve immediately. A final sprinkling of coarse salt may well come in handy.

I love this classic dish, but cooking it in the oven is time-consuming and sometimes fiddly. In the pressure cooker, it's almost instant and very easy. You can't cook more than four chicory heads at a time, but that's enough to serve four people as a side dish. If you have some about, duck fat (about two tablespoons) makes a luxurious alternative to butter.

pressure-braised chicory

serves 4

4 firm white heads of
  chicory
100ml good chicken
  stock
50g butter
salt and freshly ground
  black pepper

Remove any brown or floppy leaves from the chicory but do not trim the bases. This will help them hold together during cooking. Heat up at least 5cm water in your pressure cooker with the steamer insert (or an improvised steamer rack) in place. Put the chicory, stock, butter and seasoning in a flat-based heatproof dish that will fit in your pressure cooker with at least 2.5cm of space between the dish and the side of the pan. Clamp on the lid. Bring up to full pressure, turn the heat down to medium and cook for 5 minutes. Turn off the heat and vent immediately. Serve.

Another good way of doing chicory.

chicory with crème fraîche

serves 2

2 heads of chicory
2 tablespoons crème
   fraîche or soured cream
2 tablespoons chicken or
   vegetable stock
salt and freshly ground
   black pepper

Remove any brown or floppy leaves from the chicory but do not trim the bases. This will help them hold together during cooking. Heat up at least 5cm water in your pressure cooker with the steamer insert (or an improvised steamer rack) in place. Put the chicory in a heatproof dish that will fit in your pressure cooker with at least 2.5cm of space between the dish and the side of the pan. Spoon over the crème fraîche or soured cream and the stock, then season with salt and freshly ground black pepper. Clamp on the lid. Bring up to full pressure, turn the heat down to medium and cook for 5 minutes. Turn off the heat and vent immediately. Serve.

This vegetable is sometimes boring, but not when you cook it this way. Duck fat is the ideal; vegetable oil will do.

braised spring greens

serves 6

3 tablespoons duck fat
   or vegetable oil
6 shallots, peeled but
   left whole
12 peeled, cooked
   chestnuts
2–3 heads spring greens
   (about 1kg), trimmed,
   cored and sliced as
   thickly as you like
250ml good stock,
   chicken or vegetable
juice of ½ lemon
salt and freshly ground
   black pepper

Put the fat or oil in the pressure cooker with the shallots and chestnuts. Season well with salt and freshly ground black pepper, and cook over a moderate heat until the shallots are starting to take on some colour and smelling really good. Add the remaining ingredients, except the lemon juice, pushing down on the greens if they stick up higher than two thirds of the way up the pressure cooker walls.

Clamp on the lid. Bring up to full pressure, turn the heat down to medium and cook for 2 minutes. Turn off the heat and vent immediately if you want the greens to retain a good bit of bite. If you want them lusciously soft, leave it to vent gradually. Dump everything into a large serving bowl and toss with the lemon juice.

This is one of my favourite simple vegetable dishes.
Brief cooking mellows out the aniseed flavour and
the dressing sweetens it further.

fennel with olive oil

serves 4 as a side dish

2 large fennel bulbs,
   trimmed and halved
   or quartered
2 tablespoons chicken
   stock
2 tablespoons extra
   virgin olive oil
1 teaspoon balsamic
   vinegar
salt and freshly ground
   black pepper
coarse salt and chopped
   fennel fronds, to
   garnish (optional)

Heat up at least 5cm water in your pressure cooker with the steamer insert (or an improvised steamer rack) in place. Put the fennel in a heatproof dish that will fit in your pressure cooker with at least 2.5cm of space between the dish and the side of the pan. Add the stock and half the oil, and season with salt and freshly ground black pepper. Clamp on the lid. Bring up to full pressure, turn down the heat to medium and cook for 3 minutes (for al dente) or 5 minutes for fully soft. Turn off the heat and vent immediately. Toss with the remaining oil and the vinegar, and add a final sprinkling of coarse salt and some chopped fennel fronds if you like.

puddings

The pressure cooker can't do every type of pudding well. But what it does well, it does very, very well. At the top of my list comes steamed puddings. My friend Matthew Fort regards these as Britain's greatest contribution to world cuisine, and I am inclined to agree with him. They are perfect in the pressure cooker, identical to their long-steamed counterparts but needing much less time. There are two of them here, plus a New England variant using the same principle. Also a poached fruit recipe and a rice pudding. In all these cases, any good recipe can be adapted for use under pressure. Instead of peaches, use apples, pears, plums, nectarines, and so on. Instead of chocolate sponge, use lemon, orange or whatever you prefer. The important thing is the principle, and this is laid out here. Sweet tooths were never satisfied so speedily.

This recipe comes from Jessica Ford, who adapted it from Marguerite Patten's *Step by Step Cookery* (1964) after eating it with pleasure at her grandmother's house. It is unspeakably delicious. Jessica says: 'When we returned home after visiting my grandparents, my sister and I would badger our mother incessantly to make steamed puddings.'

chocolate steamed pudding

serves 4–6

100g slightly salted butter, plus extra for greasing

100g golden caster sugar

2 medium eggs

1 teaspoon vanilla extract

100g self-raising flour

1 tablespoon good-quality cocoa powder

2 tablespoons grated dark chocolate

about 1 tablespoon warm water

double cream, crème fraîche or a hot chocolate custard, to serve

Butter a 1.2 litre pudding basin. Cream the butter with the caster sugar until light and fluffy. Beat the eggs in a separate bowl and add gradually. Add the vanilla extract and mix in.

In the meantime, heat up at least 5cm water in your pressure cooker with the steamer insert (or an improvised steamer rack) in place.

Sift the flour and cocoa over the mixture. Gently fold, with the chocolate, into the egg and butter mixture. Add a tablespoon or so of warm water until the mixture is soft enough to drop from the spoon easily.

Pour the mixture into your prepared basin, filling only three quarters of the basin to allow room to rise. Take a double square of greaseproof paper, large enough to hang over the rim of the basin by a few centimetres, and fold a pleat into it to allow for expansion. Butter the underside, and secure the paper with a long piece of string under the rim. Loop the string over the basin and tie on the opposite side to make a handle.

Put the basin into the steamer, cover the pressure cooker without clamping the lid closed, and steam for 15 minutes. This is essential to allow the sponge to rise.

Now clamp on the lid. Bring up to full pressure, turn the heat down to medium and cook for 25 minutes. Turn off the heat and vent immediately. Remove the basin using the string handle. Run a knife around the inside of the basin and turn out on to a plate. Serve either with double cream or crème fraîche or, as in the old days, with a hot chocolate custard.

This recipe comes to me from Jessica Ford, who adapted it from Jane Grigson's *English Food*. Jessica first ate Sussex pond pudding at school in Sussex and says that 'it lived in my imagination for years afterwards. It is a glorious pudding, the more so for being so surprising.' Jessica substituted frozen and grated butter for the traditional suet. Final note: thanks to Josceline Dimbleby's *The Cooks Companion* for clarifying the pastry origami.

sussex pond pudding

serves 6

250g self-raising flour, plus extra for dusting
125g frozen butter
about 75ml milk mixed with 75ml water
1 large unwaxed lemon
100g soft light brown sugar, or a mix of soft light brown and golden caster sugar
100g butter, cut into pieces, plus extra for greasing
double cream or crème fraîche, to serve

Butter a 1 litre pudding basin well. Measure the flour into a large bowl and grate the frozen butter straight over it. Mix in with a knife rather than your fingers so that the warmth from your fingers won't soften the butter too quickly. Gradually add enough milk and water to form a soft dough. Gather the dough into a ball and leave for a few moments to rest, then gently roll it out into a large circle. Cut one quarter of the circle out (think of a clock face and cut out 12.00–3.00) and put to one side. This will be the lid. Carefully lift the remaining dough and use to line the pudding basin. Press the cut sides together to make a clean join.

Wash the lemon and prick it deeply all over with a metal skewer. Put half the sugar into the basin, followed by half the butter cut into pieces. Put the lemon on top, then add the remaining sugar and butter. Roll out the remaining dough to make a lid. Place on top of the pudding basin. Trim or fold it if there is too much.

Butter a double layer of greaseproof paper. With butter side in, fold a pleat in the middle and cover the top of the basin. Cover with foil and secure with string under the rim. Loop the string over the basin and tie on the opposite side to make a handle.

Heat up at least 5cm water in your pressure cooker with the steamer insert (or an improvised steamer rack) in place. Put the basin into the steamer, cover the pressure cooker without clamping the lid closed, and steam for 15 minutes. This is essential to allow the sponge to rise.

Now clamp on the lid. Bring up to full pressure, turn the heat down to medium and cook for 30 minutes. Turn off the heat and vent immediately. Remove the basin using the string handle. Run a knife around the inside of the basin and carefully and quickly turn out on to a plate. Cut a piece of the lemon to serve to each person. Serve with double cream or crème fraîche.

steamed pudding variations

There are dozens of great steamed puddings in the British repertoire, and there's no reason not to adapt them for use in the pressure cooker. You can try one of the following, substituting the relevant ingredients for the cocoa powder, dark chocolate and vanilla in the chocolate pudding recipe.

ginger/cinnamon pudding
1 teaspoon powdered ginger
2 thick slices fresh ginger, peeled and finely chopped
1 teaspoon cinnamon powder

jam pudding
2 tablespoons raspberry or strawberry jam

Put the jam in the bottom of the basin, distributing it evenly, then put the sponge on top.

marmalade pudding
2 tablespoons marmalade jam

Put the jam in the bottom of the basin, distributing it evenly, then put the sponge on top.

orange pudding
Juice and grated zest of 1 orange

lemon pudding
Juice and grated zest of 1 lemon

This is based on a recipe in *The United States Regional Cook Book*, edited by Ruth Berolzheimer (1947). It can also be made using blackberries or cranberries; if using cranberries, add an extra 50g of sugar.

new england blueberry pudding

serves 6

125g plain flour
1½ teaspoons baking powder
½ teaspoon salt
125g butter, cut into small pieces, plus extra for greasing
25g dried breadcrumbs
100g granulated sugar
1 egg, beaten
150ml milk
250g blueberries
crème fraîche or cream, to serve

Butter a 1 litre or 1.5 litre pudding basin. Sift the flour, baking powder and salt into a large bowl. Mix in the butter using two knives, then add the breadcrumbs and sugar, and mix well. Finally, stir in the egg and milk, blend well, then gently stir in the blueberries.

Pour the mixture into your prepared basin, filling only three quarters of the basin to allow room to rise. Take a double square of greaseproof paper, large enough to hang over the rim of the basin by a few centimetres, and fold a pleat into it to allow for expansion. Butter the underside, and secure the paper with a long piece of string under the rim. Loop the string over the basin and tie on the opposite side to make a handle.

Heat up at least 5cm water in your pressure cooker with the steamer insert (or an improvised steamer rack) in place. Put the basin into the steamer, cover the pressure cooker without clamping the lid closed, and steam for 15 minutes. This is essential to allow the sponge to rise.

Now clamp on the lid. Bring up to full pressure, turn the heat down to medium and cook for 35 minutes. Turn off the heat and vent immediately. Remove the basin using the string handle.

Run a knife around the inside of the basin and turn out on to a plate. Serve with crème fraîche or cream if you wish.

This is an ultra-simple version which can be jazzed up in whatever way you like. It's good served with raspberry or strawberry jam, if you really want to push the sugar-boat out.

rice pudding

serves 4

200ml rice

600ml milk, preferably
   full fat

4 tablespoons granulated
   sugar

50–100g raisins or
   sultanas

½ teaspoon ground
   cinnamon

2 tablespoons double
   cream

Put all the ingredients, except the cream, in a bowl that will fit into your steamer with at least 2.5cm of space between the bowl and the side of the pan. Clamp on the lid. Bring up to full pressure, turn the heat down to medium and cook for 15 minutes. Turn off the heat and leave to vent gradually. Left in the pressure cooker, the pudding will stay warm for a good 20 minutes or so. Just before serving, stir in the cream.

Ruthie Falconer, who inspired this recipe, serves them with honey and crème fraîche. If you don't want the extra sweetness from the honey, they are good just with crème fraîche or double cream.

ms falconer's pressure-poached peaches

serves 4

200ml water or rosé
    wine
1 scrap of cinnamon
    stick
1 clove
2 cardamom pods
4 peaches, of a good
    colour but not too soft,
    halved and stoned
2–3 tablespoons golden
    granulated sugar
honey and crème fraîche,
    to serve

Heat the water or wine and the spices gently for a few minutes, either by microwaving in the dish you will use for steaming or in a small pan. Heat up at least 5cm water in your pressure cooker with the steamer insert (or an improvised steamer rack) in place. Put all the ingredients in a heatproof dish that will fit into your steamer with at least 2.5cm of space between the dish and the side of the pan.

Put the dish into the steamer. Clamp on the lid. Bring up to full pressure, turn the heat down to medium and cook for 6–7 minutes, or 8–9 if you want the peaches meltingly soft. Turn off the heat and vent immediately. Leave to cool, and serve with honey and crème fraîche passed separately.

fruit puddings

Poached fruit is one of my favourite desserts for simple, informal dinner parties: they take so little time to prepare, and the active cooking is a breeze. When peaches are out of season (i.e., outside late summer and early autumn), make this dish with some suggested alternatives:

Pears with Port
Apples with Cider
Golden Plums with Muscat
Purple Plums with Port

index

T

V

Additional photo credits:

p.30 © eli_asenova/iStock
p.85 © Anton Ignatenco/iStock
p.98 © Alasdair Thomson/iStock
p.123 © arnaud weisser/iStock

acknowledgements

As always, my first thanks go to everyone at Kyle Cathie Books, the best publisher any cookery writer could ask for. Special thanks to my editor, Catharine Robertson.

The photographs in this book are the result of a remarkable collaboration, which is hard to explain and doesn't always receive due credit, between three people. Sue Rowlands learned what the food was going to look like and chose the settings in which it would be presented, from backgrounds to serving vessels to forks, spoons and knives. Jane Lawrie cooked the food and assembled it on Sue's canvas. Will Heap took what these two gifted women presented, and turned that raw material (if you'll pardon the expression) into photographs of rare beauty which also convey the essence of each dish. He describes himself as 'just the guy that presses the button once everyone else has worked tirelessly to come up with something new and inventive.' That's unduly modest, but there is an element of truth in his description. My heartfelt and humble thanks to all of them, and to Mark Latter, who designed the book beautifully.

Special thanks to various people for their advice and help of various sorts. I have adapted numerous recipes from other cookery writers for use in the pressure cooker, and I thank them – all cited in the recipes – for their expertise. John Whiting, a pressure cooker of long experience, shared his views with me. Jessica Ford provided pressure cooked pudding recipes for me to use, as did Celia Dodd.

Special thanks to Tefal UK, who supplied me with the pressure cooker that first got me started with this wonderful cooking method – and which serves me well to this day. Thanks also to Slice PR, who organised the loan of a brand-new Tefal pressure cooker for photography. And finally, thanks to Sharon Boundy of UK Guinea Fowl (www.ukguineafowl.co.uk), who sent – at short notice – beautiful feathers for photography.

As always, I thank my wife, Emma Dally, and my daughters Rebecca, Alice and Ruth. They tasted the sometimes rotten fruits of my labours, and made helpful comments when things went wrong. And special thanks to my old friend Jane Walker, who often stayed with my wife and me during the testing of recipes. She ate many of my experiments, and usually liked them.